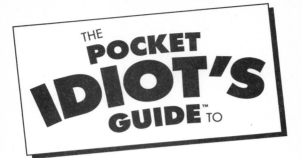

Spanish for Law Enforcement Professionals

by Lieutenant Jacquelyn R. MacConnell

D1572644

ALPHA

A member of Penguin Group (USA) Inc.

This book is dedicated to law enforcement personnel around the world. May we continue to learn and grow in our professions. May we also continue to remain compassionate through our careers regardless of the evil we see every day.

ALPHA BOOKS

Published by the Penguin Group

Penguin Group (USA) Inc., 375 Hudson Street, New York, New York 10014, USA

Penguin Group (Canada), 90 Eglinton Avenue East, Suite 700, Toronto, Ontario M4P 2Y3, Canada (a division of Pearson Penguin Canada Inc.)

Penguin Books Ltd., 80 Strand, London WC2R 0RL, England

Penguin Ireland, 25 St. Stephen's Green, Dublin 2, Ireland (a division of Penguin Books Ltd.)

Penguin Group (Australia), 250 Camberwell Road, Camberwell, Victoria 3124, Australia (a division of Pearson Australia Group Pty. Ltd.)

Penguin Books India Pvt. Ltd., 11 Community Centre, Panchsheel Park, New Delhi—110 017, India

Penguin Group (NZ), 67 Apollo Drive, Rosedale, North Shore, Auckland 1311, New Zealand (a division of Pearson New Zealand Ltd.)

Penguin Books (South Africa) (Pty.) Ltd., 24 Sturdee Avenue, Rosebank, Johannesburg 2196, South Africa

Penguin Books Ltd., Registered Offices: 80 Strand, London WC2R 0RL, England

International Standard Book Number: 978-1-59257-784-2
Library of Congress Catalog Card Number: 2008922780

10 09 08   8 7 6 5 4 3 2 1

Interpretation of the printing code: The rightmost number of the first series of numbers is the year of the book's printing; the rightmost number of the second series of numbers is the number of the book's printing. For example, a printing code of 08-1 shows that the first printing occurred in 2008.

Printed in the United States of America

Note: This publication contains the opinions and ideas of its author. It is intended to provide helpful and informative material on the subject matter covered. It is sold with the understanding that the author and publisher are not engaged in rendering professional services in the book. If the reader requires personal assistance or advice, a competent professional should be consulted.

The author and publisher specifically disclaim any responsibility for any liability, loss, or risk, personal or otherwise, which is incurred as a consequence, directly or indirectly, of the use and application of any of the contents of this book.

Most Alpha books are available at special quantity discounts for bulk purchases for sales promotions, premiums, fund-raising, or educational use. Special books, or book excerpts, can also be created to fit specific needs.

For details, write: Special Markets, Alpha Books, 375 Hudson Street, New York, NY 10014.

Contents

Introduction

The primary goal of this book is to make you safer while protecting the public, because knowing even basic Spanish during the critical moments law enforcement professionals encounter every day could save a life—your partner's, an innocent bystander's, or your own.

In addition, this book was written to help law enforcement professionals communicate with the Spanish-speaking public. The following pages provide vocabulary and phrases that can be used to gather basic information for determining what type of crime occurred and completing a basic report.

Don't be embarrassed or discouraged if you're not able to speak Spanish with an accent. When people from other countries speak English, they speak with an accent. When you speak Spanish, you will, more than likely, have an American accent. Don't let this concern or deter you. The more you use the language, the more familiar you'll become with the words and phrases—and that's what's important.

Keep in mind that each Spanish-speaking country uses slightly different vocabulary and has different accents. In comparison, think of American English and an American accent compared to Scottish English and a Scottish accent. Although the vocabulary used in this book is generally understood regardless of the Spanish-speaking country of origin, it's always important to remember that one word can mean two different things to two different nationalities.

Extras

Throughout the book, you'll see special boxes of information to add to your learning. Here's what to look for:

Check these boxes for tips about using Spanish to communicate.

Heed these warnings and pitfalls about certain words and/or phrases.

Find common slang specific to the law enforcement community in these boxes.

Acknowledgments

Many people assisted me throughout my career and in continuing to develop my Spanish skills. A few friends I'd like to mention include Mariana de la Fuente, who is always there when I need her for Spanish questions; Detective Icela Brown, who helped me start the Spanish program for the Phoenix Police Department and who is a constant inspiration; Lennys Toth and Detective Ed

Martinez, who have taken time out of their busy schedules to assist me with my business; and last but not least, my parents, for their lifelong support.

Special Thanks to the Technical Reviewer

The Pocket Idiot's Guide to Spanish for Law Enforcement Professionals was reviewed by an expert who double-checked the accuracy of what you'll learn here, to help us ensure that this book gives law enforcement professionals everything they need to know about Spanish on the job. Special thanks are extended to Ana Brignoni-Walczek.

Trademarks

All terms mentioned in this book that are known to be or are suspected of being trademarks or service marks have been appropriately capitalized. Alpha Books and Penguin Group (USA) Inc. cannot attest to the accuracy of this information. Use of a term in this book should not be regarded as affecting the validity of any trademark or service mark.

Spanish Basics

In This Chapter

- Learning your Spanish ABCs (*ah-beh-sehs*)
- Pronouncing Spanish letters like a pro
- Spanish cognates
- Takin' it to the street

If you're brand new to Spanish, you've come to the right place. In this first chapter, we start out with the very basics of the Spanish language, beginning with the alphabet and pronunciation of specific letters and combinations. Sometimes you will see the same word with the option of two endings, for example *hijo* (*EE-hoh*) versus *hija* (*EE-hah*). This indicates masculine (ending in *-o* most of the time) versus feminine (ending in *-a* most of the time). When I refer to the masculine and feminine of objects, this only refers to the object itself, not to who it belongs. For example, the word for a dress tie, *la corbata* (*lah kohr-BAH-tah*) is a feminine word in Spanish, it is an object, but it is commonly used by males.

We also look at words that look the same in Spanish as they do in English, dialects, *Spanglish*, and slang. We've got a lot to cover, so let's go!

The Spanish Alphabet

Unlike in English, where some letters in words are silent or unpronounced, when you read Spanish, you generally pronounce each letter of the word (although there are some exceptions). So it's important to know how to pronounce each letter in Spanish. To make it easier, sometimes the translations sound a lot like their English equivalent, as you'll see in the following table.

An uneducated Spanish speaker will sometimes refer to Y as *ya* or *yeh*. He or she might not even know of the formal and correct *ee-gree-eh-gah*.

The Spanish Alphabet

Letter	Spanish	Pronunciation	English
A (*ah*)	accidente	*ahx-ee-DEHN-teh*	accident
	arrestar	*ah-rehs-TAHR*	to arrest
B (*beh*)	bala	*BAH-lah*	bullet
	barba	*BAHR-bah*	beard
C (*seh*)	cajuela	*kah-boo-WEH-lah*	trunk of a car
	¿cómo?	*KOH-moh*	what? how?
CH (*cheh*)	choque	*CHOH-keh*	accident, vehicle related
	chota	*CHOH-tah*	cop (*slang*)
D (*deh*)	drogas	*DROH-gahs*	drugs
	dinero	*dee-NEH-roh*	money
E (*eh*)	estrangular	*ehs-trahn-goo-LAHR*	to strangle
	emergencia	*eh-mehr-HEHN-see-ah*	emergency

continues

The Spanish Alphabet (continued)

Letter	Spanish	Pronunciation	English
F (*efe*)	familia	*fah-MEE-lee-ah*	family
	fallecer	*fah-yeh-SEHR*	to pass away, die
G (*heh*)	ganga	*GAHN-gah*	gang (*slang*)
	golpear	*gohl-peh-AHR*	to hit
H (*ache*)	hijo/hija	*EE-hoh/EE-hah*	son/daughter
	hombre	*OHM-breh*	man
I (ee)	ilegal	*ee-leh-GAHL*	illegal
	inocente	*ee-noh-SEHN-teh*	innocent
J (*hota*)	jura	*HOO-rah*	police (*slang*)
	jueves	*hoo-EH-vehs*	Thursday
K (*kah*)	kilómetro	*kee-LOH-mee-troh*	kilometer
	kilo	*KEE-loh*	kilogram
L (*ele*)	levantar	*leh-vahn-TAHR*	to raise, lift
	licencia	*lee-SEHN-see-ah*	license

Letter	Spanish	Pronunciation	English
M (*emeh*)	maltratar	*mahl-trah-TAHR*	mistreat
	mota	*MOH-tah*	marijuana (*slang*)
N (*eneh*)	negro	*NEH-groh*	black (color)
	nombre	*NOHM-breh*	name
Ñ (*enyeh*)	daño	*DAHN-nyoh*	damage
	años	*AH-nyohs*	years
O (*oh*)	oscuro	*oh-SKOO-roh*	dark
	oficial	*oh-fee-see-AHL*	officer, official
P (*peh*)	patrulla	*pah-TROO-yah*	patrol
	pandilla	*pahn-DEE-yah*	gang
Q (*coo*)	¿quién?	*kee-EHN*	who?
	querido	*keh-REE-doh*	lover, loved one
R (*ereh*)	robar	*roh-BAHR*	to rob
	rodillas	*roh-DEE-yahs*	knees

continues

The Spanish Alphabet (continued)

Letter	Spanish	Pronunciation	English
RR (*erreh*)	carro	*KAHR-roh*	car
	versus		
	caro	*KAH-roh*	expensive
	perro	*PEHR-roh*	dog
	versus		
	pero	*PEH-roh*	but
S (*eseh*)	sangre	*SAHN-greh*	blood
	suéltelo	*SWEHL-teh-loh*	drop it
T (*teh*)	tribunal	*tree-boo-NAHL*	court (court of law)
	testigo	*tehs-TEE-goh*	witness
U (*oo*)	uniforme	*oo-nee-FOHR-meh*	uniform
	urgencia	*oor-HEN-see-yah*	urgency, urgent need
V (*veh*)	violación	*vee-oh-lah-see-OHN*	sexual assault, violation
	viejo	*vee-EH-hoh*	old

Letter	Spanish	Pronunciation	English
W (*doble oo*) or (*doble veh*)	whisky	*WEE-skee*	whisky
	waterpolista	*wah-tehr-poh-LEES-tah*	water polo player
X (*eh-kees*)	(Few words start with X)		
	México/ Méjico	*Meh-HEE-koh*	Mexico
	Texas/Tejas	*TEH-hahs*	Texas
	Xavier/Javier	*hah-vee-EHR*	man's name
Y (*ee-gree-eh-gah*)	yo	*yoh*	I
	yerno	*YEHR-noh*	son-in-law
Z (*setah*)	zapatos	*sah-PAH-tohs*	shoes

Spanish Pronunciation Tips

The preceding table gave you some general pronunciation tips, but you do need to know a few more things about Spanish pronunciation before you turn to the next chapter on vocabulary. The following tips will help you pronounce letters and combinations of letters of the Spanish alphabet that are often misunderstood.

B Versus *V*

The Spanish *B* (*beh*) and *V* (*veh*) sound a lot alike. When talking to a suspect or victim, the difference might be important, so you can ask some questions to help distinguish between the two similar-sounding letters. Ask "*¿B de burro o V de vaca?*" (*beh deh BOOR-roh oh veh deh VAH-kah*; *B* from the word *burro* or *V* from the word *vaca?*). You can also try "*¿B grande o v chica?*" (*beh GRAHN-deh oh veh CHEE-kah*; The big *B* or the little *v?*). This reference is made because a *B* is bigger than a *V*.

Pronouncing *H*

H (*ache*) is silent except when with *c*: *ch* = *cheh*.

hotel	hospital
oh-TEHL	*ohs-pee-TAHL*
hotel	hospital

Pronouncing *J*

J (*hota*) in words makes an English *h* sound:

jura	jale
HOO-rah	*HAH-leh*
swearing in, to pledge	pull

Jura is also slang for "police," and *jale* is slang for a "job."

Pronouncing *LL*

LL together makes an English *y* sound: *llaves* = *YAH-vehs* (keys). Other words with the *ll* are:

lluvia	llorar
YOO-vee-ah	*yoh-RAHR*
rain	to cry

Pronouncing *Ñ*

Ñ (*enyeh*) makes the same sound as the letter *n* in the English word *canyon*. Pronouncing the *ñ* when it's present in a word is very important. *N* (*eneh*) versus *ñ* (*enyeh*) can make all the difference:

ano	año
AH-noh	*AHN-nyoh*
anus	year

Pronouncing *QU*

QU always has an English *k* sound: *quemadura* =
keh-mah-DOO-rah (burn). In Spanish, the English *k*
sound is always spelled with *qu* followed by either *e*
or *i*. The letter *k* in Spanish is actually a borrowed
letter, just like *w*.

queso	quince
KEH-soh	*KEEN-seh*
cheese	fifteen

Pronouncing *X*

X (*eh-kees*) is sometimes pronounced with an
English *h* sound. For example, *Texas* (spelled the
same in Spanish) is pronounced *TEH-hahs*. If the
origination of the word is from the Nahuatl language (another language from Mexico), like *Texas*,
Oaxaca, or *México*, the *x* is pronounced with an
English *h* sound. However, more often *X* takes
on a hard English *x* sound, as in *éxito* (success),
pronounced *ehx-EE-toh*, and *excelente* (excellent),
pronounced *ehx-seh-LEHN-teh*.

Pronouncing *Z*

Z (*setah*) often takes on an English *s* sound in
Spanish. For example, *zapatos* (shoes) is pronounced
sah-PAH-tohs; zacate (grass) is pronounced *sah-
KAH-teh;* and *zanahoria* (carrot) is pronounced *sah-
nah-OH-ree-ah*.

Keep it Simple

Some words are commonly spelled with either a *z* or *s. Gutierrez/Gutierres, Hernandez/Hernandes,* and *Ramirez/ Ramires* are some common examples. Be sure to verify the spelling when you're taking statements. Ask, "*¿Con seta o esay?*" (*¿Kohn SEH-tah oh EH-seh?;* with a "*z*" or "*s*"?).

GU Pronunciation Variations

The Spanish combination *GU* has a few important pronunciation rules you should be aware of:

GU followed by an *i* or an *e* = silent *u*:

guitarra	guerra
gee-TAHR-rah	*GEHR-rah*
guitar (*u* is not pronounced)	war (*u* is not pronounced)

When *GU* is followed by an *a* or a consonant, pronounce all the letters:

Gutierrez	guardar
goo-tee-EHR-rehz	*goo-AHR-dahr*
last name (hard *g* sound, pronounce all letters)	to guard, to keep, watch over (hard *g* sound, pronounce all letters)

Normally, *gua* makes an English *w* sound:

> guapo
> *goo-AH-poh* or *gwapo*
> handsome

When *G* is followed by an *e* or *i*, pronounce the *g* with English *h* sound:

> gente
> *HEN-teh*
> people

> gigante
> *hee-GAHN-teh*
> giant

G followed by an *a*, *o*, or *u* makes a hard *g* sound:

> gato
> *GAH-toh*
> cat

> golpear
> *gohl-peh-AHR*
> to hit

> gusto
> *GOOS-toh*
> taste, pleasure

GU with a dierisis or *gü* makes a definitive *gw* sound:

> pingüino
> *peen-GWEE-noh*
> penguin

> bilingüe
> *bee-LEENG-gway*
> bilingual

Pronouncing Vowels

Probably the most important thing to remember about the pronunciation of vowels in Spanish is that the vowels do *not* change pronunciation based on the word they're in. They're always the same sound: *A* = *ah*, *E* = *eh*, *I* = *ee*, *O* = *oh*, and *U* = *oo*.

despacio
dehs-PAH-see-oh
slow

regresar
reh-greh-SAHR
return

murciélago
moor-see-EHL-ah-goh
bat

In these examples, the *E* always makes an *eh* sound.

Let's look at the word for glove: *guante* = *GWAN-teh*. If we break this down further, you can hear the pronunciation of each vowel: *goo-AHN-teh*. When you're having a hard time pronouncing a word, break it down after the vowels:

ametralladora
ah-meh-trah-yah-DOH-rah
machine gun

nacionalidad
nah-see-oh-nah-lee-DAHD
nationality

Words That Look the Same

Cognates are words that look the same in English as they do in other languages. They often have the same meaning (lucky for you!) but not always.

Cognates

Spanish	Pronunciation	English
acusado	*ah-koo-SAH-doh*	accused
escapar	*ehs-kah-PAHR*	escape
familia	*fah-MEE-lee-ah*	family
reformar	*reh-fohr-MAHR*	reform
registrar	*reh-hee-STRAHR*	register; search or inspect
violación	*vee-oh-lah-see-OHN*	violation; sexual assault

Stop Sign Until you become proficient in Spanish, to be safe and to be sure you're understood, stay away from using *violación* for anything other than sexual assault.

Be aware of *false* cognates. These are words that look the same in English and Spanish but have very different translations:

éxito
EXH-ee-toh
success (*not* exit)

crimen
KREE-mehn
murder (*not* crime)

noticias
noh-TEE-see-ahs
the news (*not* notice)

Spanish Is Spanish Is Spanish ... Isn't It?

The Spanish spoken in various Spanish-speaking countries is often quite different. The people's accents and the vocabulary used are especially noticeable. An Argentinean accent, for example, is different from a Cuban, Mexican, or Colombian accent.

And sometimes, the same word can have quite different meanings in different Spanishes. For example, *cabrón/cabrona* (*kah-BROHN/kah-BROH-nah*) literally means "billy goat," "bastard," or "bitch." Mexicans sometimes use this word jokingly with someone they're familiar with. But to a Cuban or Puerto Rican, this word is often used in a much more serious name-calling fashion and is not taken lightly.

Street Spanish is what you'll most likely encounter in everyday contacts with the public and in investigations. It's usually specific to a certain geographical area, be it a city or even a neighborhood. The differences might not be noticeable in all cases, but some might leave you scratching your head.

Spanglish

Spanglish is the combination of Spanish and English to create a word similar to its English equivalent.

liquear   chequear
lee-kee-AHR   *cheh-keh-AHR*
to leak   to check

mopear

moh-peh-AHR

to mop

> **Stop Sign**
>
> Spanglish is sometimes thought of as the words English speakers create by adding *o* to the end of any word to create a supposed Spanish word: *chair-o, table-o, floor-o*. Don't fall into this stereotype.

Spanish Slang

Like English, Spanish has slang words, and depending on how they're used, they change meaning. For example, *ponte trucha* (*POHN-teh TROO-chah*) literally means "put" and "trout," but it's slang for "be aware" or "be careful." Likewise, *ponte agua* (*POHN-teh AH-gwah*) means "put" and "water," but together, the words are slang for "be aware."

Throughout the book, I include the slang words with the straight translations so you'll know better what you're hearing on the street.

Helpful Phrases

I gave you a lot of information in this first chapter. You might not remember everything during your first interactions with Spanish speakers, and that's okay. For quick reference when you need help, the following phrases are good ones to have handy when you meet a Spanish speaker.

My name is _____.
Mi nombre es _____.
Mee NOHM-breh ehs _____.

I am a police officer.
Yo soy un/una oficial.
Yoh soi oon/OO-nah oh-fee-see-AHL.

Thank you
Gracias
GRAH-see-ahs

Excuse me
Perdóneme
Pehr-DOH-neh-meh

Come here please.
Venga aquí por favor.
VEHN-gah ah-KEE pohr fah-VOHR.

Common Vocabulary

In This Chapter

- Learning the numbers in Spanish
- What color?
- Telling time and the date
- Family and friends, names and occupations
- Which way do I go?

Now that you have the Spanish alphabet and some pronunciation tips down from Chapter 1, it's on to some Spanish vocabulary you need to know. Whether you're soliciting information or having a general conversation, the information in this chapter will definitely come in handy. In the following pages, we look at the Spanish words for numbers, days of the week, months of the year, colors, common jobs, common locations, and friends and family members.

One, Two, Three: Numbers

Numbers in Spanish are fairly easy; think of it like this: for numbers 16 through 19, the exact translation of the Spanish equivalent is "ten and …." So *dieciséis* (*dee-ehs-ee-SEH-ehs*) exactly translates to "ten and six" (think of it as *diez y seis*), or sixteen.

The same translation occurs with *veinte* (*VEHN-teh*; twenty) through *noventa* (*noh-VEHN-tah*; ninety); for example, *sesenta y uno* (*seh-SEHN-tah ee OO-noh*) exactly translates to "sixty and one," or sixty-one; *ochenta y uno* (*oh-CHEHN-tah ee OO-noh*) exactly translates to "eighty and one," or eighty-one.

When using a number before a noun, for example "one car," use *un carro* (*oon KAHR-roh*). Use *un* for all masculine nouns and *una* for all feminine nouns. For example, "one house" is *una casa* (*OO-nah KAH-sah*).

The same thing applies when you get into the hundreds. For example, "two hundred cars" is *doscientos carros* (*dohs-see-EHN-tohs KAHR-rohs*) and "two hundred houses" is *doscientas casas* (*dohs-see-EHN-tahs KAH-sahs*). For all the other numbers, feminine and masculine are not differentiated.

Numbers

English	Spanish	Pronunciation
(0) zero	cero	*SEH-rob*
(1) one	uno	*OO-nob*
(2) two	dos	*dobs*
(3) three	tres	*trebs*
(4) four	cuatro	*KWAH-trob*
(5) five	cinco	*SEEN-kob*
(6) six	seis	*SEH-ebs*
(7) seven	siete	*see-EH-teb*
(8) eight	ocho	*OH-chob*
(9) nine	nueve	*noo-EH-veb*
(10) ten	diez	*dee-EHS*
(11) eleven	once	*OHN-seb*

continues

Numbers (continued)

English	Spanish	Pronunciation
(12) twelve	doce	*DOH-seh*
(13) thirteen	trece	*TREH-seh*
(14) fourteen	catorce	*kah-TOHR-seh*
(15) fifteen	quince	*KEEN-seh*
(16) sixteen	dieciséis	*dee-ehs-ee-SEH-ehs*
(17) seventeen	diecisiete	*dee-eh-see-see-EH-teh*
(18) eighteen	dieciocho	*dee-eh-see-OH-choh*
(19) nineteen	diecinueve	*dee-eh-see-noo-EH-veh*
(20) twenty	veinte	*VEHN-teh*
(30) thirty	treinta	*TREHN-tah*
(40) forty	cuarenta	*kwah-REHN-tah*
(50) fifty	cincuenta	*seen-KWEHN-tah*
(60) sixty	sesenta	*seh-SEHN-tah*

English	Spanish	Pronunciation
(70) seventy	setenta	*seh-TEHN-tah*
(80) eighty	ochenta	*oh-CHEHN-tah*
(90) ninety	noventa	*noh-VEHN-tah*
(100) one hundred	cien	*see-EHN*
(200) two hundred	doscientos	*dohs-see-EHN-tohs/tahs*
(300) three hundred	trescientos	*trehs-see-EHN-tohs/tahs*
(400) four hundred	cuatrocientos	*kwah-troh-see-EHN-tohs/tahs*
(500) five hundred	quinientos	*kee-nee-EHN-tohs/tahs*
(600) six hundred	seiscientos	*seh-ehs-see-EHN-tohs/tahs*
(700) seven hundred	setecientos	*seh-teh-see-EHN-tohs/tahs*
(800) eight hundred	ochocientos	*oh-choh-see-EHN-tohs/tahs*
(900) nine hundred	novecientos	*noh-veh-see-EHN-tohs/tahs*
(1,000) one thousand	mil	*meel*

Here's an interesting fact: in Spanish, four-digit numbers use periods instead of commas, as in English use. So for 1,000, you'd write 1.000.

All the Colors of the Rainbow

One important thing to remember about Spanish colors: when the gender of what you're referring to changes, so does the end of the word, and that includes colors. For example, *negro* (*NEH-groh*) and *negra* (*NEH-grah*), both mean "black," but the gender of what's being referenced has changed— *negro* being masculine and *negra* being feminine.

What color was it?
¿Qué color era?
¿keh koh-LOHR EH-rah?

Stop Sign

The color gold is *dorado* (*doh-RAH-doh*), but the metal gold is *oro* (*OH-roh*). The color silver is *plateado* (*plah-teh-AH-doh*), but the metal silver is *plata* (*PLAH-tah*). Be sure to keep the two straight!

Colors

English	Spanish	Pronunciation
black	negro	*NEH-groh*
blue	azul	*ah-SOOL*
brown	café/marrón	*kah-FEH/mahr-ROHN*
copper	cobre/cobrizo	*KOH-breh/koh-BREE-soh*
dark red/burgundy	guinda	*GEEN-dah*
gold	dorado	*doh-RAH-doh*
gray	gris	*grees*
green	verde	*VEHR-deh*
lead gray/dark gray	plomo	*PLOH-moh*
light blue	celeste	*seh-LEHS-teh*
navy blue	azul marino	*ah-SOOL mah-REE-noh*
orange	anaranjado	*ah-nah-rahn-HAH-doh*

continues

Colors (continued)

English	Spanish	Pronunciation
pink	rosa	*ROH-sah*
purple	morado	*moh-RAH-doh*
red	rojo	*ROH-hoh*
silver	plateado	*plah-teh-AH-doh*
violet	violeta	*vee-oh-LEH-tah*
white	blanco	*BLAHN-koh*
yellow	amarillo	*ah-mah-REE-yoh*

What Time Is It?

You need to know how to say the time in Spanish or understand it when spoken to you. After all, when asking someone what time an incident occurred, you need to understand their response. Let's try to make this easy.

What time is it?
¿Qué hora es?
¿keh OH-rah ehs?

One o'clock is referred to in the singular (*es*) format:

It is one.
Es la una.
ehs lah OO-nah.

It happened at one.
Ocurrió a la una.
oh-koo-ree-OH ah lah OO-nah.

The times from two o'clock through twelve o'clock take a plural (*son*) format:

It is two.
Son las dos.
sohn lahs dohs.

It is twelve.
Son las doce.
sohn lahs DOH-seh.

When giving the time, say the hour and then the minutes for up until 30 minutes after the hour:

It is three twenty.
Son las tres y veinte.
sohn lahs trehs ee VEHN-tah.

It is eleven twenty-five.
Son las once y veinticinco.
sohn lahs OHN-seh ee vehn-tee-SEEN-koh.

For quarter past the hour and half past the hour, the following are commonly used:

It is four and a half. *Or:* **It is four thirty.**
Son las cuatro y media.
sohn lahs KWAH-troh ee MEH-dee-ah.

It is seven and a quarter. *Or:* **It is seven fifteen.**
Son las siete y cuarto.
sohn lahs see-EH-teh ee KWAHR-toh.

For thirty through fifty-nine past the hour, these are the common translations:

It is five minus eleven. *Or:* **It is four forty-nine.**
Son las cinco menos once.
sohn lahs SEEN-koh MEH-nohs OHN-seh.

It is eight minus twenty-five. *Or:* **It is seven thirty-five.**
Son las ocho menos veinticinco.
sohn lahs OH-choh MEH-nohs vehn-teh-SEEN-koh.

When talking about morning or night, the following are commonly used:

It is two in the morning.
Son las dos de la mañana.
sohn lahs dohs deh lah mahn-NYAH-nah.

It is two in the afternoon.
Son las dos de la tarde.
sohn lahs dohs deh lah TAHR-deh.

The following phrases are helpful when talking about a time of day:

Last night
Anoche
ah-NOH-cheh

In the morning
En la mañana *Or:* Por la mañana
ehn lah mahn-NYAH-nah Or: *Pohr lah mahn-NYAH-nah*

This morning
Esta mañana
EHS-tah mahn-NYAH-nah

Tonight
Esta noche
EHS-tah NOH-cheh

 The word *mañana*, depending on how it's used, can mean morning or a coming day. Pay attention to how the word is used and in what context.

The Months of the Year

With the exception of January, all the months have essentially the same base in Spanish as they do in English: *mayo* (*MAH-yoh*) is May, *marzo* (*MAHR-soh*) is March, *septiembre* (*sep-tee-EHM-breh*) is September. Even if you didn't know they had the same base, you could probably match these up. Let's look at all the months.

Which month?
¿Qué mes?
¿KEH mehs?

Months

English	Spanish	Pronunciation
January	enero	*eh-NEH-roh*
February	febrero	*feh-BREH-roh*
March	marzo	*MAHR-soh*
April	abril	*ah-BREEL*
May	mayo	*MAH-yoh*
June	junio	*HOO-nee-yoh*
July	julio	*HOO-lee-oh*
August	agosto	*ah-GOHS-toh*
September	septiembre	*sep-tee-EHM-breh*
October	octubre	*ohk-TOO-breh*
November	noviembre	*noh-vee-EHM-breh*
December	diciembre	*dee-see-EHM-breh*

The Days of the Week

The days of the week are important to know, but so are words that make reference to different days of the week. You might get a response as simple as "Tuesday," but you might also get something like "the day after tomorrow."

Day of the week?
¿Día de la semana?
¿DEE-ah deh lah seh-MAH-nah?

Days of the Week

English	Spanish	Pronunciation
Monday	lunes	*LOO-nehs*
Tuesday	martes	*MAHR-tehs*
Wednesday	miércoles	*mee-EHR-koh-lehs*
Thursday	jueves	*hoo-EH-vehs*
Friday	viernes	*bee-EHR-nehs*
Saturday	sábado	*SAH-bah-doh*
Sunday	domingo	*doh-MEEN-goh*

The following words and phrases are used when referencing days of the week.

References to Days

English	Spanish	Pronunciation
the next	el próximo, la próxima	*ehl PROHX-ee-moh, lah PROHX-ee-mah*
the next Saturday	el próximo sábado	*ehl PROHX-ee-moh sah-BAH-doh*
tomorrow	mañana	*mahn-NYAH-nah*
yesterday	ayer	*AH-yehr*
the day before (literally "before yesterday")	antes de ayer	*AHN-tehs deh AH-yehr*
the day after tomorrow (literally "past tomorrow")	pasado mañana	*pah-SAH-doh mahn-NYAH-nah*
this	este	*ehs-teh*

English	Spanish	Pronunciation
this Thursday	este jueves	*EHS-teh hoo-EH-vehs*
this coming	que viene	*keh vee-EH-neh*
the upcoming Monday	el lunes que viene	*ehl LOO-nehs keh vee-EH-neh*
past	pasado	*pah-SAH-doh*
the past Sunday	el domingo pasado	*ehl doh-MEEN-goh pah-SAH-doh*

Friends and Family

To establish relationships among subjects, you need to know the words for different family members. The following table lists the terms for some of the common relationships.

Friends and Family Members

English	Spanish	Pronunciation
male friend	amigo	*ah-MEE-goh*
female friend	amiga	*ah-MEE-gah*
boyfriend	novio	*NOH-vee-oh*
girlfriend	novia	*NOH-vee-ah*
Slang:	ruca	*ROO-kah*
husband	esposo	*ehs-POH-soh*
wife	esposa	*ehs-POH-sah*
ex-husband	ex-esposo	*ehx-ehs-POH-soh*
ex-wife	ex-esposa	*ehx-ehs-POH-sah*
brother	hermano	*ehr-MAH-noh*
sister	hermana	*ehr-MAH-nah*
son	hijo	*EE-hoh*
daughter	hija	*EE-hah*
father	padre	*PAH-dreh*
mother	madre	*MAH-dreh*
grandfather	abuelo	*ah-BWEH-loh*
grandmother	abuela	*ah-BWEH-lah*
grandson	nieto	*nee-EH-toh*
granddaughter	nieta	*nee-EH-tah*
god son	ahijado	*ah-ee-HAH-doh*

English	Spanish	Pronunciation
god daughter	ahijada	*ah-ee-HAH-dah*
male cousin	primo	*PREE-moh*
female cousin	prima	*PREE-mah*
uncle	tío	*TEE-oh*
aunt	tía	*TEE-ah*
nephew	sobrino	*soh-BREE-noh*
niece	sobrina	*soh-BREE-nah*
brother-in-law	cuñado	*koo-NYAH-doh*
sister-in-law	cuñada	*koo-NYAH-dah*
father-in-law	suegro	*SWEH-groh*
mother-in-law	suegra	*SWEH-grah*
son-in-law	yerno	*YEHR-noh*
daughter-in-law	nuera	*noo-EH-rah*

Understanding Hispanic Surnames

Most Latin cultures use both paternal and maternal last names along with first names, oftentimes not having a middle name per se:

Luis Carlos   Lopez   Rodriguez
(first name)   *(paternal)*   *(maternal)*

Ana Teresa   Manzo   de Castillo
(first name)   *(paternal)*   *(husband's last name)*

When asking for a last name, specify the paternal last name, maternal last name, or both. When Luis Carlos Lopez Rodriguez becomes "Americanized," he will most likely go by Luis Lopez. When Ana Teresa Manzo de Castillo becomes Americanized, she will mostly likely go by Ana Castillo.

What Do You Do?

When obtaining someone's information, you'll probably also ask what his or her occupation is. The following table lists some common jobs or occupations you might hear in response.

What do you do for work?
¿En qué trabaja?
¿ehn KEH trah-BAH-hah?

Common Jobs

English	Spanish	Pronunciation
baker	panadero/a	*pah-nah-DEH-roh/rah*
boss	patrón/jefe	*pah-TROHN/HEH-feh*
butcher	carnicero/a	*kahr-nee-SEH-roh/rah*
cashier	cajero/a	*kah-HEH-roh/rah*
construction	construcción	*kohn-strook-see-OHN*
cook	cocinero/a	*koh-see-NEH-roh/rah*
doctor	doctor/a	*dohk-TOHR/TOH-rah*
electrician	electricista	*eh-lehk-tree-SEES-tah*
employee	empleado/a	*ehm-pleh-AH-doh/dah*
engineer	ingeniero/a	*een-hehn-ee-EH-roh/rah*

English	Spanish	Pronunciation
entrepreneur	empresario/a	*ehm-preh-SAH-ree-oh/ah*
gardener	jardinero	*hahr-dee-NEH-roh*
landscaper	los jardines	*lohs hahr-DEE-nehs*
lawyer	abogado/a	*ah-boh-GAH-doh/dah*
mechanic	mecánico	*meh-KAH-nee-koh*
musician	músico	*MOO-see-koh*
roofer	techador	*teh-chah-DOHR*
nurse	enfermero/a	*ehn-fehr-MEH-roh/rah*
painter	pintor/a	*peen-TOHR/TOH-rah*
pastor	pastor/a	*pas-TOHR/TOH-rah*
plumber	plomero/ra	*ploh-MEH-roh/rah*
reporter	periodista	*peh-ree-oh-DEES-tah*
salesperson	vendedor/ra	*vehn-deh-DOHR/DOH-rah*
teacher	maestro/a	*mah-EHS-troh/trah*
technician	técnico/a	*TEHK-nee-koh/kah*
waiter	mesero	*meh-SEH-roh*
waitress	mesera	*meh-SEH-rah*
yard worker	jardinero/a	*hahr-dee-NEH-roh/rah*

Location, Location, Location

Jobs/occupations sometimes correspond with the Spanish word for a location. For example, the word for butcher is a *carnicero* (*kahr-nee-SEH-roh*) and he or she works at the meat store or *carnicería* (*kahr-nee-seh-REE-ah*); a baker or *panadero* (*pah-nah-DEH-roh*) works at the bakery or *panadería* (*pah-nah-deh-REE-ah*).

A location might also be referred to when talking about where someone works or someone's destination or location. Although there are many more words referencing locations, the following table lists a few you might hear.

Locations

English	Spanish	Pronunciation
apartment	apartamento	*ah-pahr-tah-MEHN-toh*
bakery	panadería	*pah-nah-deh-REE-ah*
bank	banco	*BAHN-koh*
clothing store	tienda de ropa	*tee-EHN-dah deh ROH-pah*
condominium	condominio	*kohn-doh-MEE-nee-oh*
dance club	discoteca	*dees-koh-TEH-kah*
food store	mercado	*mehr-KAH-doh*
home	casa	*KAH-sah*
meat store	carnicería	*kahr-nee-seh-REE-ah*
pharmacy	farmacia	*fahr-mah-SEE-ah*
restaurant	restaurante	*rehs-tau-RAHN-teh*
sport club	club deportivo	*cloob deh-pohr-TEE-voh*
store (small)	tienda	*tee-EHN-dah*
supermarket	supermercado	*soo-pehr-mehr-KAH-doh*
yard	jardín	*hahr-DEEN*

Which Way?: Directions

You need to know which way is which when you're taking a statement or giving directions to a Spanish speaker. The words in the following table help with both.

Directions

English	Spanish	Pronunciation
right	derecha	*deh-REH-chah*
left	izquierda	*ees-kee-EHR-dah*
straight	derecho	*deh-REH-choh*
east	este	*EHS-teh*
west	oeste	*oh-EHS-teh*
north	norte	*NOHR-teh*
south	sur	*soor*
northeast	noreste	*nohr-EHS-teh*
northwest	noroeste	*nohr-oh-EHS-teh*
southeast	sureste	*soor-EHS-teh*
southwest	suroeste	*soor-oh-EHS-teh*
street	calle *Or:* carretera	*KYE-yeh Or:* *kahr-reh-TEH-rah*
avenue	avenida	*ah-veh-NEE-dah*
block	cuadra	*KWAH-drah*

Helpful Phrases

This chapter contained a lot of general vocabulary. Here are some phrases to tie all the information together:

One number at a time
Un número a la vez
oon NOO-meh-roh ah lah vehs

Your Social Security number, one number at a time
Su seguro social, un número a la vez
soo seh-GOO-roh soh-SEE-ahl, oon NOO-meh-roh ah lah vehs

What time did it occur?
¿A qué hora ocurrió?
¿ah KEH OH-rah oh-koor-ree-OH?

Are you married?
¿Está casado/a?
¿ehs-TAH kah-SAH-doh/dah?

Is he/she your son/daughter?
¿Es él/ella su hijo/hija?
¿ehs ehl/eyah soo EE-hoh/EE-hah?

Is he/she your blood relative?
¿Es él/ella su pariente directo?
¿ehs ehl/eyah soo pah-ree-EHN-teh dee-REHK-toh?

What is his/her relationship to you?
¿Cuál es su parentezco con usted?
¿KWAHL ehs soo pah-rehn-TEHS-koh kohn oo-STEHD?

3

Just the Facts

In This Chapter

- Do we have any witnesses?
- How about your personal information?
- Obtaining a suspect's information and description

If you're not proficient in Spanish, it's best to keep questions and interviews to a minimum, focusing on the facts only. The more complex a conversation is, the better your understanding must be of the language. With that in mind, let's forge ahead and learn some closed-ended questions that will require a short response.

Understanding What Happened

When investigating any incident, use closed-ended questions and stay away from questions like "*¿Que pasó?*" (*keh pah-SOH;* "What happened?"). By using closed-ended questions, the answers will be shorter and more precise, and easier for you to understand.

Try to obtain a minimal amount of information to accurately determine what type of crime is being investigated.

Working With Witnesses

Regardless of the crime, having a witness is very useful. The following questions enable you to determine not only if someone is a witness, but whether they will be able to provide pertinent information to the investigation.

Did anyone see anything?
¿Alguien vio algo?
¿AHL-gee-ehn VEE-oh AHL-goh?

Are you a witness?
¿Es usted un testigo?
¿ehs oo-STEHD oon tehs-TEE-goh?

Did you see what happened?
¿Vio lo que pasó?
¿VEE-oh loh keh pah-SOH?

Would you be willing to testify in court?
¿Está dispuesto/a a testificar en los tribunales/la corte?
¿ehs-TAH dees-PWEHS-toh/tah ah tehs-tee-fee-KAHR ehn lohs tree-boo-NAH-lehs/lah KOHR-teh?

Can you describe the suspect?
¿Puede describir al sospechoso?
¿PWEH-deh dehs-kree-BEYR ahl sohs-peh-CHOH-soh?

Do you know the victim?
¿Conoce a la víctima?
¿koh-NOH-seh ah lah VEEK-tee-mah?

Do you know the suspect?
¿Conoce al sospechoso?
¿koh-NOH-seh ahl sohs-peh-CHOH-soh?

Obtaining Personal Information

Be specific when asking for someone's information. Ask for "complete name" rather than just "name." Nicknames are commonplace in the Hispanic community and are important to obtain as well as a complete name.

Here are some phrases that might come in handy when dealing with obtaining personal information:

Do you have a license or identification?
¿Tiene licencia o identificación?
¿tee-EH-neh lee-SEHN-see-ah oh ee-dehn-tee-fee-kah-see-OHN?

If he or she has a license or identification with an address listed, point to the information and ask "¿Correcto?" (*kohr-REHK-toh*; "Correct?").

What is your name, complete name?
¿Cómo se llama, nombre completo?
¿KOH-moh seh YAH-mah, NOHM-breh kohm-PLEH-toh?

How do you spell it?
¿Cómo se escribe?
¿KOH-moh seh ehs-KREE-beh?

If you're expecting the subject to provide a middle name, don't. Sometimes they don't have what Americans consider a "middle name." To clarify what information you're asking for, ask "*¿Nombre, apellido paterno, apellido materno?*" (*¿NOHM-breh, ah-peh-YEE-doh pah-TEHR-noh,, ah-peh-YEE-doh mah-TEHR-noh?*; "Name, paternal last name, maternal last name?").

Your nickname?
¿Su apodo/sobrenombre?
¿soo ah-POH-doh/soh-breh-NOHM-breh?

When were you born?
¿Cuándo nació?
¿KWAHN-doh nah-see-OH?

Date of birth?
¿Fecha de nacimiento?
¿FEH-chah deh nah-see-mee-EHN-toh?

Your Social Security number?
¿Su número de seguro social?
¿soo NOO-meh-roh deh seh-GOO-roh soh-see-AHL?

Your exact address? (of your house)
¿Su dirección exacta? (del domicilio)
¿soo dee-rehk-see-OHN ehx-AHK-tah? (dehl doh-mee-SEE-lee-oh)

Apartment or house?
¿Apartamento o casa?
¿ah-pahr-tah-MEHN-toh oh KAH-sah?

City and state?
¿Ciudad y estado?
¿see-oo-DAHD ee ehs-TAH-doh?

Zip code?
¿Código postal?
¿KOH-dee-goh pohs-TAHL?

Telephone number? (the area code?)
¿Número de teléfono? (¿el areá?)
¿NOO-meh-roh deh teh-LEH-foh-noh? (¿ehl ah-REH-ah?)

Where do you work?
¿Dónde trabaja?
¿DOHN-deh trah-BAH-hah?

Name of your employer?
¿Nombre de su empleo?
¿NOHM-breh deh soo ehm-PLEH-oh?

The exact address?
¿La dirección exacta?
¿lah dee-rehk-see-OHN ehx-AHK-tah?

How tall are you? (in feet and inches)
¿Cuánto mide? (en pies y pulgadas)
¿KWAHN-toh MEE-deh? (ehn PEE-ehs ee pool-GAH-dahs)

How much do you weigh? (in pounds)
¿Cuánto pesa? (en libras)
¿KWAHN-toh peh-sah? (ehn LEE-brahs)

Latin countries use the metric system. 2.2 pounds equals 1 kilogram, and 0.3 meters equals 1 foot.

Obtaining a Suspect Description

Obtaining information on a known suspect is much easier than obtaining information on an unknown suspect. The following questions are designed to obtain important, possibly future identifying characteristics.

When It's a Known Suspect

Obtaining information on a known suspect is easier because you'll most likely be able to obtain pertinent information. So first and foremost, let's find out if they know the suspect. Then proceed with obtaining more information.

Do you know the suspect?
¿Conoce al sospechoso?
¿koh-NOH-seh ahl sohs-peh-CHOH-soh?

What is his/her name, complete name?
¿Cómo se llama él/ella, nombre completo?
*¿KOH-moh seh YAH-mah ehl/EY-yah NOHM-breh
kohm-PLEH-toh?*

Name, paternal last name, maternal last name?
¿Nombre, apellido paterno, apellido materno?
*¿NOHM-breh, ah-peh-YEE-doh pah-TEHR-noh,
ah-peh-YEE-doh mah-TEHR-noh?*

Does he/she have a nickname?
¿Tiene apodo/sobrenombre?
¿tee-EH-neh ah-POH-doh/soh-breh-NOHM-breh?

How old is he/she?
¿Cuántos años tiene?
¿KWAHN-tohs AHN-nyos tee-EH-neh?

Do you know when he/she was born? Date of birth?
¿Sabe cuándo nació él/ella? ¿Fecha de nacimiento?
¿SAH-beh KWAHN-doh nah-see-OH ehl/eyah?
¿FEH-chah deh nah-see-mee-EHN-toh?

Do you know his/her Social Security number?
¿Sabe el seguro social de él/ella?
*¿SAH-beh ehl seh-GOO-roh soh-see-AHL deh ehl/
eyah?*

Do you know where he/she lives? (their house)
¿Sabe dónde vive él/ella? (el domicilio)
*¿SAH-beh DOHN-deh VEE-veh ehl/eyah? (ehl doh-
mee-SEE-lee-oh)*

The exact address? (their house)
¿La dirección exacta? (del domicilio)
¿lah dee-rehk-see-OHN ehx-AHK-tah? (dehl doh-mee-SEE-lee-oh)

STOP SIGN People from foreign countries sometimes aren't used to providing physical addresses, so don't be surprised if the person you're talking to cannot provide his or her exact address.

Do you know his/her telephone number?
¿Sabe el número de teléfono de él/ella?
¿SAH-beh ehl NOO-meh-roh deh teh-LEH-foh-noh deh ehl/eyah?

Do you know where he/she works?
¿Sabe dónde trabaja él/ella?
¿SAH-beh DOHN-deh trah-BAH-hah ehl/eyah?

Name of employer? (Refers to an organization.)
¿Nombre del empleo?
¿NOHM-breh dehl ehm-PLEH-oh?

Name of his/her boss?
¿Nombre de su jefe?
¿NOHM-breh deh soo HEH-feh?

When It's an Unknown Suspect

With an unknown suspect, you need to be prepared to obtain a complete physical description. The questions are extensive, and you might be able to scale them down depending on your situation.

Was the suspect light- or dark-skinned?
¿El sospechoso era de piel clara o oscura?
¿Ehl sohs-peh-CHOH-soh EH-rah deh pee-EHL KLAH-rah oh ohs-KOO-rah?

Skin Color

English	Spanish	Pronunciation
Dark-skinned	Piel oscura	*pee-EHL ohs-KOO-rah*
Light-skinned	Piel clara	*pee-EHL KLAH-rah*
	huero/güero	*WEH-roh*

Could you tell the suspect's nationality?
¿Sabe la nacionalidad del sospechoso?
¿SAH-beh lah nah-see-oh-nah-lee-DAHD dehl sohs-peh-CHOH-soh?

Nationalities

English	Spanish	Pronunciation
African American/ black/dark skin	negro/a	NEH-groh/grah
American	americano/a	ah-meh-ree-KAH-noh/nah
Argentinean	argentino/a	ahr-hehn-TEE-noh/nah
Asian	asiático/a	ah-see-AH-tee-koh/kah
Bolivian	boliviano/a	boh-lee-vee-AH-noh/nah
Chilean	chileno/a	chee-LEH-noh/nah
Chinese	chino/a	CHEE-noh/nah
Colombian	colombiano/a	koh-lohm-bee-AH-noh/nah
Costa Rican	costarricense	kohs-tahr-ree-SEHN-seh
Cuban	cubano/a	koo-BAH-noh/nah
Dominican	dominicano/a	doh-mee-nee-KAH-noh/nah
Ecuadorian	ecuatoriano/a	eh-kwah-toh-ree-AH-noh/nah
Guatemalan	guatemalteco/a	gwah-teh-mahl-TEH-koh/kah

English	Spanish	Pronunciation
Honduran	hondureño/a	*ohn-doo-REHN-nyoh/nyah*
Japanese	japonés/a	*hah-poh-NEHS/NEHS-sah*
Korean	coreano/a	*koh-reh-AH-noh/nah*
Latin	latino/a	*lah-TEE-noh/nah*
Mexican	mexicano/a	*meh-bee-KAH-noh/nah*
Mexican, U.S. born	pocho/a	*POH-choh/chah*
	moreno/a	*moh-REH-noh/nah*
Mexican American	méxico americano/a	*meh-bee-koh-ah-mehr-ee-KAH-noh/nah*
Nicaraguan	nicaragüense	*nee-kah-rah-GWEHN-seh*
Panamanian	panameño/a	*pah-nah-MEH-nyoh/nyah*
Paraguayan	paraguayo/a	*pah-rah-goo-AH-yoh/yah*
Peruvian	peruano/a	*peh-roo-AH-noh/nah*
Philippine	filipino/a	*fee-lee-PEE-noh/nah*

continues

Nationalities (continued)

English	Spanish	Pronunciation
Puerto Rican	puertorriqueño/a	*pwehr-toh-ree-KEH-nyoh/nyah*
Salvadorian	salvadoreño/a	*sahl-vah-doh-REH-nyoh/nyah*
Spanish	español/a	*ehs-pah-NYOHL/ehs-pah-NYOH-lah*
Uruguayan	uruguayo/a	*oo-roo-goo-AH-yoh/yah*
U.S.-born Mexican	chicano/a	*chee-KAH-noh/nah*
Venezuelan	venezolano/a	*veh-neh-soh-LAH-noh/nah*

How old was the suspect?
¿Cuántos años tiene el sospechoso?
¿KWAHN-tohs AHN-nyos tee-EH-neh ehl sohs-peh-CHOH-soh?

Age Identification

English	Spanish	Pronunciation
more or less	más o menos	*mahs oh MEH-nohs*
old	viejo	*vee-EH-hoh*
elderly person	anciano/a	*ahn-see-AH-noh/nah*
young	joven	*HOH-vehn*
adolescent/teenager	adolescente	*ah-doh-leh-SEHN-teh*
middle-aged man	hombre maduro	*OHM-breh mah-DOO-roh*
middle-aged woman	mujer madura	*moo-HEHR mah-DOO-rah*

Was the suspect fat or skinny?
¿El sospechoso era gordo o flaco?
¿ehl sohs-peh-CHOH-soh EH-rah GOHR-doh oh FLAH-koh?

Their body type?
¿Qué tipo de cuerpo?
¿KEH TEE-poh deh KWEHR-poh?

Body Types

English	Spanish	Pronunciation
skinny	flaco	*FLAH-koh*
thin	delgado	*dehl-GAH-doh*
medium	mediano	*meh-dee-AH-noh*
fat	gordo/ panzón	*GOHR-doh/ pahn-SOHN*
muscular	musculoso	*moos-koo-LOH-soh*
chubby man	relleno	*reh-YEH-noh*
chubby woman	rellena	*reh-YEH-nah*

In Spanish, when the ending *-ito* is added to a word, for example, "fat" is *gordo* (*GOHR-doh*), but *gordito* (*gohr-DEE-toh*) is used to refer to someone as a little bit fat, and *gordita* (*gohr-DEE-tah*) would refer to a female. The *-ito/-ita* can be added on to any of the descriptors.

How much did he/she weigh?
¿Cuánto pesa él/ella?
¿KWAHN-toh PEH-sah ehl/eyah?

How tall was he/she? (in feet and inches)
¿Cuánto mide él/ella? (en pies y pulgadas)
¿KWAHN-toh MEE-deh ehl/eyah? (ehn PEE-ehs ee pool-GAH-dahs)

Street Slang The response to the "How tall was he/she?" question is usually either *alto* (*AHL-toh;* tall) or *bajo* (*BAH-hoh;* short). Another word for short is *chaparro*, which usually means "very short."

What was his/her hair color?
¿Color de pelo?
¿koh-LOHR deh PEH-loh?

Hair Colors

English	Spanish	Pronunciation
black	negro	*NEH-groh*
blond	rubio	*ROO-bee-oh*
brown	café	*kah-FEH*
brunette	castaño	*kahs-TAHN-nyoh*
colored	teñido/ pintado	*teh-NYEE-doh/ peen-TAH-doh*
gray	canoso	*kah-NOH-soh*
red	rojo/ pelirrojo	*ROH-hoh/ peh-lee-ROH-hoh*

What type of hair did the suspect have?
¿Qué tipo de pelo tenía el sospechoso?
¿KEH TEE-poh deh PEH-loh teh-NEE-ah ehl sohs-peh-CHOH-soh?

Types of Hair

English	Spanish	Pronunciation
Bald	Pelón	*peh-LOHN*
Braids	Trenzas	*TREHN-sahs*
Curly hair	Pelo rizado	*PEH-loh ree-SAH-doh*
	Pelo chino	*PEH-loh CHEE-noh*
Long hair	Pelo largo	*PEH-loh LAHR-goh*
Short hair	Pelo corto	*PEH-loh KOHR-toh*
Ponytail	Cola/cola de caballo	*KOH-lah/KOH-lah deh kah-BAH-yoh*
Straight hair	Pelo lacio	*PEH-loh LAH-see-oh*
Wavy hair	Pelo ondulado	*PEH-loh ohn-doo-LAH-doh*

To find out whether a suspect has facial hair, ask
"*¿Tenía barba?*" (*¿teh-NEE-ah BAHR-bah?*) and
"*¿Tenía bigote?*" (*¿teh-NEE-ah bee-GOH-teh?*). These
translate to "Did he have a beard?" and "Did he
have a mustache?"

Facial Hair

English	Spanish	Pronunciation
Beard	Barba	*BAHR-bah*
Goatee	Chivo/candado	*CHEE-voh/kahn-DAH-doh*
Mustache	Bigote	*bee-GOH-teh*
Sideburns	Patillas	*pah-TEE-yahs*
Well shaven	Bien afeitado	*BEE-ehn ah-feh-TAH-doh*

Did he/she speak English or Spanish?
¿Habló inglés o español?
¿ah-BLOH een-GLEHS o ehs-pah-NYOHL?

Did the suspect have an accent?
¿Tenía acento?
¿teh-NEE-ah ah-SEHN-toh?

Voice Characteristics

English	Spanish	Pronunciation
Accent	Acento	*ah-SEHN-toh*
Bad pronunciation	Mala pronunciación	*MAH-lah proh-noon-see-ah-see-OHN*
Loud voice	Voz alta	*vohs AHL-tah*
Quiet voice	Voz baja	*vohs BAH-hah*

Did he/she have a tattoo?
¿Tenía tatuaje?
¿teh-NEE-ah tah-too-AH-heh?

What did it look like?
¿Cómo era?
¿KOH-moh EH-rah?

Tattoo Types

English	Spanish	Translation
Animal	Animal	*ah-nee-MAHL*
Letters	Letras	*LEH-trahs*
Numbers	Números	*NOO-meh-rohs*
Picture	Un dibujo o foto	*oon dee-BOO-hoh o FOH-toh*
Symbol	Un símbolo	*oon SEEM-boh-loh*

Did he/she have a scar?
¿Tenía cicatriz?
¿teh-NEE-ah see-kah-TREESE?

Did he/she have moles?
¿Tenía lunares?
¿teh-NEE-ah loo-NAH-rehs?

Did he/she have freckles?
¿Tenía pecas?
¿teh-NEE-ah PEH-kahs?

Helpful Phrases

Here are some useful phrases to use at the beginning stages of gathering information:

Speak slowly, please.
Hable despacio, por favor.
AH-bleh dehs-PAH-see-oh, pohr fah-VOHR.

I speak a little Spanish.
Hablo poco español.
AH-bloh POH-koh ehs-pahn-NYOHL.

Did he/she have any identifying characteristics?
¿Tenía alguna característica especial?
¿teh-NEE-ah ahl-GOO-nah kah-rahk-teh-REES-tee-kah ehs-peh-see-AHL?

Repeat, please.
Repita por favor.
reh-PEE-tah pohr fah-VOHR.

The same as
Igual que
ee-GWAHL keh

For example:
The same as me.
Igual que yo.
ee-GWAHL keh yoh.

The same as him/her.
Igual que él/ella.
ee-GWAHL keh EHL/eyah.

4

Medical Emergencies

In This Chapter

- Traffic accidents
- Accidents around pools
- Poisonings
- Heart attacks and other emergencies
- The baby is on its way!

This chapter includes basic vocabulary helpful when responding to a variety of medical emergency situations, from traffic accidents and falls—to delivering a baby!

Traffic Accidents

For a general traffic accident, you only need to know if someone is injured and where. For more complicated situations, you need to be able to obtain information to help however you can until medical personnel arrive.

Do you need medical attention? Yes or no?
¿Necesita atención médica? ¿Sí o no?
¿neh-seh-SEE-tah ah-tehn-see-OHN MEH-dee-kah?
¿see oh noh?

Where are you hurt?
¿Adónde está golpeado?
¿ah-DOHN-deh ehs-TAH gohl-peh-AH-doh?

The phrase *enséñeme dónde* (*ehn-seh-NYAH-meh DOHN-deh*; show me where) is helpful when asking a question like "Where are you hurt?" The subject can simply point to where they're injured.

When a Person's Trapped in a Vehicle

When a person is trapped in a vehicle after an auto accident, the situation can be frightening for everyone involved. Here's how to ask the right questions and get the information you need to help.

Are you trapped?
¿Está atrapada?
¿ehs-TAH ah-trah-PAH-dah?

What part of your body is trapped?
¿Qué parte de su cuerpo está atrapado?
¿KEH PAHR-teh deh soo KWEHR-poh ehs-TAH ah-trah-PAH-doh?

Where do you hurt?
¿Dónde le duele?
¿DOHN-deh leh DWEH-leh?

Can you feel sensation in your arms/legs/ fingers/toes?
¿Puede sentir sus brazos/piernas/dedos/dedos de los pies?
¿PWEH-deh sehn-TEER soos BRAH-sohs/pee-EHR-nahs/DEH-dohs/DEH-dohs deh lohs pee-EHS?

Do not move. Medics are on their way.
No se mueva. Los paramédicos estan en camino.
noh seh moo-EH-vah. lohs pah-rah-MEH-dee-kohs ehs-TAHN ehn kah-MEE-noh.

Stay calm.
Cálmese.
KAHL-meh-seh.

Is/was there anyone else in the vehicle?
¿Hay/Había alguien más en el vehículo?
¿ai/ah-BEE-ah AHL-gee-ehn MAHS ehn ehl veh-HEE-koo-loh?

You never know what might happen in a traffic accident, so be sure to ask if anyone else is or was in the vehicle. Someone could have been thrown from the car.

I have to get you out of the vehicle.
Tengo que sacarlo/la del vehículo.
TEHN-goh keh sah-KAHR-loh/lah dehl veh-HEE-koo-loh.

Hold on to me while I pull.
Sosténgase de mí mientras jalo.
sohs-TEHN-gah-seh deh MEE mee-EHN-trahs HAH-loh.

Hold on to my arm while I pull.
Tómese de mi brazo mientras jalo.
TOH-meh-seh deh MEE BRAH-soh mee-EHN-trahs HAH-loh.

Drowning/Near Drowning

Drownings or near drownings can occur at a public location or in someone's own backyard. The more information you're able to get from the people on the scene, the better you can assist medical personnel when they arrive.

How long was he/she in the water?
¿Cuánto tiempo estuvo él/ella en el agua?
¿KWAHN-toh tee-EHM-poh ehs-TOO-voh EHL/ eyah ehn ehl AH-gwah?

Was he/she floating face down?
¿Estaba flotando boca abajo?
¿ehs-TAH-bah floh-TAHN-doh BOH-kah ah-BAH-hoh?

Did you perform CPR?
¿Le hizo respiración boca a boca?
¿leh EE-soh rehs-pee-rah-SEE-ohn BOH-kah ah BOH-kah?

How long has it been since his/her last breath?
¿Cuánto tiempo hizo desde su último respiro?
¿KWAHN-toh tee-EHM-poh EE-soh DEHS-deh soo
OOL-tee-moh rehs-PEE-roh?

How old is he/she?
¿Cuántos años tiene él/ella?
¿KWAHN-tohs AH-nyohs tee-EH-neh EHL/eyah?

Falls

No matter the age of the victim, falls can be dangerous situations. Here's how to gather information
and respond to the victim and others present.

Questions for Victims

If the victim is conscious, he or she will be able to
provide details about the accident. Obtain as much
information as you can so you can provide the best
service possible.

Where did you fall from?
¿Usted de dónde se cayó?
¿oo-STEHD deh DOHN-deh seh kah-YOH?

How long ago did this occur?
¿Hace cuánto tiempo pasó?
¿AH-seh KWAHN-toh tee-EHM-poh pah-SOH?

Did you hit your head?
¿Usted se golpeó la cabeza?
¿oo-STEHD seh gohl-peh-OH lah kah-BEH-sah?

Did you lose consciousness?
¿Usted perdió el conocimiento?
¿oo-STEHD pehr-dee-OH ehl koh-noh-see-mee-EHN-toh?

For how long?
¿Por cuánto tiempo?
¿pohr KWAHN-toh tee-EHM-poh?

Are you bleeding anywhere?
¿Está usted sangrando?
¿ehs-TAH oo-STEHD sahn-GRAHN-doh?

Where are your injuries from this fall?
¿Dónde tiene las heridas de la caída?
¿DOHN-deh tee-EH-neh lahs eh-REE-dahs deh lah kah-EE-dah?

Do you feel like anything is broken?
¿Siente que tiene algo roto?
¿see-EHN-teh keh tee-EH-neh AHL-goh ROH-toh?

Questions for Witnesses

Witnesses are very important in this type of situation, especially if the victim is unable to provide answers. These questions will help assess the victim's status.

Where did he/she fall from?
¿De dónde se cayó?
¿deh DOHN-deh seh kah-YOH?

Did he/she hit his/her head?
¿Se golpeó la cabeza?
¿Seh gohl-pee-OH lah kah-BEH-sah?

Did he/she lose consciousness?
¿Perdió el conocimiento?
¿Pehr-dee-OH ehl koh-noh-see-mee-EHN-toh?

Is he/she bleeding anywhere?
¿Está sangrando?
¿Ehs-TAH sahn-GRAHN-doh?

Do you know what injuries were sustained from the fall?
¿Sabe qué heridas fueron ocacionadas por la caída?
¿SAH-beh KEH eh-REE-dahs FWEH-rohn oh-kah-see-oh-NAH-dahs pohr lah kah-EE-dah?

Poisoning

Ideally, if you respond to a call where someone has ingested poison, the victim will be able to respond to some very important questions. These questions will help determine the exigency and type of treatment.

Questions for Victims

Hopefully, if you have to respond to a call where someone has ingested some type of poison, as there are many types, they will be able to respond to some questions.

Do you know what was ingested/swallowed?
¿Sabe lo que se tragó?
¿SAH-beh loh keh seh trah-GOH?

Show me the container.
Muéstreme el frasco.
moo-EHS-treh-meh ehl FRAHS-koh.

How long ago was it ingested?
¿Hace cuánto tiempo se lo tragó?
¿AH-seh KWAHN-toh tee-EHM-poh seh loh trah-GOH?

Have you taken anything since ingesting the poison?
¿Usted tomó algo después de tomar el veneno?
¿oo-STEHD toh-MOH AHL-goh dehs-PWEHS deh toh-MAHR ehl veh-NEH-noh?

Have you been vomiting?
¿Usted ha vomitado?
¿oo-STEHD ah voh-mee-TAH-doh?

Questions for Witnesses

In the worst-case scenario, which we always prepare for, the victim won't be able to answer any questions. In that case, we hope for the best—a witness who can answer some questions for us.

Has he/she taken anything since ingesting the poison?
¿Tomó algo después de ingerir el veneno?
¿toh-MOH AHL-goh dehs-PWEHS deh een-heh-REER ehl veh-NEH-noh?

Has he/she been vomiting?
¿El/Ella ha vomitado?
¿ehl/eyah ah voh-mee-TAH-doh?

Heart Attacks

Unfortunately, people of all ages can have heart problems. With that in mind, you need to obtain information pertinent to victims of all ages.

Questions for Victims

If you're lucky enough to be able to arrive or assist prior to the victim losing consciousness, there are some very important questions that need to be asked.

Do you have a history of heart problems?
¿Usted tiene antecedentes de problemas cardíacos/ problemas del corazón?
¿oo-STEHD tee-EH-neh ahn-teh-seh-DEHN-tehs deh proh-BLEH-mahs kahr-DEE-ah-kohs/proh-BLEH- mahs dehl koh-rah-SOHN?

Do you have pain in your chest?
¿Tiene usted dolor de pecho?
¿tee-EH-neh oo-STEHD doh-LOHR deh PEH-choh?

Do you have pain in your arms?
¿Tiene dolor en sus brazos?
¿tee-EH-neh doh-LOHR ehn soos BRAH-sohs?

Show me where your pain is.
Muéstreme donde tiene el dolor.
moo-EHS-treh-meh DOHN-deh tee-EH-neh ehl doh- LOHR.

Are you short of breath?
¿Tiene dificultad al respirar?
¿tee-EH-neh dee-fee-kool-TAHD ahl rehs-pee-RAHR?

How long ago was the first pain?
¿Hace cuánto tuvo el primer dolor?
¿AH-seh KWAHN-toh TOO-voh ehl pree-MEHR doh-LOHR?

Are you on medication?
¿Está usted tomando medicamentos?
¿ehs-TAH oo-STEHD toh-MAHN-doh meh-dee-kah-MEHN-tohs?

If you have the medicine bottle with you, can I see it please?
Si tiene el frasco de medicamentos, ¿lo puedo ver, por favor?
see tee-EH-neh ehl FRAHS-koh deh meh-dee-kah-MEHN-tohs, ¿loh PWEH-doh vehr, pohr fah-VOHR?

Questions for Witnesses

As in other situations, ideally you'll be able to obtain information from both the victim and a witness(es). However, if that's not possible, you need to be prepared.

Does he/she have a history of heart problems?
¿Tiene él/ella antecedentes de problemas cardíacos/problemas del corazón?
¿tee-EH-neh ehl/eyah ahn-teh-seh-DEHN-tehs deh proh-BLEH-mahs kahr-DEE-ah-kohs/proh-BLEH-mahs dehl koh-rah-SOHN?

Did he/she grab at his/her chest?
¿Se agarró del pecho?
¿seh ah-gahr-ROH dehl PEH-choh?

Is he/she on medication?
¿Está tomando medicamentos?
¿ehs-TAH toh-MAHN-doh meh-dee-kah-MEHN-tohs?

Street Slang
Heart attacks can happen to people of nearly every age, but they're more common in the elderly. An older person may be referred to as *el viejo* (*ehl vee-EH-hoh*) or *la vieja* (*lah vee-EH-hah*), meaning the "old guy" or "old lady," respectively.

Broken Bones

Having a broken bone is a serious injury, especially depending on what's broken. Some basic rules apply when talking to a victim who might have this type of injury—most importantly, keep them from moving.

Do not move.
No se mueva.
noh seh moo-EH-vah.

What do you think is broken?
¿Qué piensa que se rompió?
¿KEH pee-EHN-sah keh seh rohm-pee-OH?

Body Parts

English	Spanish	Pronunciation
arm(s)	brazo(s)	*BRAH-soh(s)*
back	espalda	*ehs-PAHL-dah*
feet	pies	*pee-EHS*
fingers	dedos	*DEH-dohs*
hands	manos	*MAH-nohs*
knees	rodillas	*roh-DEE-yahs*
leg(s)	pierna(s)	*pee-EHR-nahs*
neck	cuello	*KWEH-yoh*
nose	nariz	*nah-REESE*
toes	dedos del pie	*DEH-dohs dehl pee-EH*

Severed Limbs

In a drastic emergency situation, a victim might lose a limb. This could happen in several instances, such as a car accident or a workplace injury. Again, some basic actions will increase the likelihood of saving the victim's life.

We have to stop the bleeding.
Tenemos que parar la pérdida de sangre.
teh-NEH-mohs keh PAH-rahr lah PEHR-dee-dah deh SAHN-greh.

I am going to tie this around your arm/leg.
Voy a atar esto alrededor de su brazo/pierna.
voi ah ah-TAHR EHS-toh ahl-reh-deh-DOHR deh soo BRAH-soh/pee-EHR-nah.

Hold your arm up.
Mantenga su brazo arriba.
mahn-TEHN-gah soo BRAH-soh ahr-REE-bah.

We need to elevate your arm/leg.
Necesitamos elevar su brazo/pierna.
neh-seh-see-TAH-mohs eh-leh-VAHR soo BRAH-soh/
pee-EHR-nah.

Burns

When assisting someone who's been burned, it's
important to know what type of burn the victim
is suffering from. From there, you will hopefully
know how to treat the burn.

How did you burn yourself?
¿Cómo se quemó?
¿KOH-moh seh keh-MOH?

Liquid/chemical/electrical/fire induced
Líquido/químicos/electricidad/fuego
LEE-kee-doh/KEE-mee-kohs/eh-lehk-tree-see-DAHD/
foo-EH-goh

When did you burn yourself?
¿Cuándo se quemó?
¿KWAHN-doh seh keh-MOH?

Where are you burned?
¿Dónde se quemó?
¿DOHN-deh seh keh-MOH?

What have you done to treat the burn?
¿Qué hizo para curar la quemadura?
¿KEH EE-soh PAH-rah koo-RAHR lah keh-mah-DOO-rah?

If you put something on the burn, show me what it was.
Si puso algo sobre la quemadura, muéstreme lo que fue.
see POO-soh AHL-goh SOH-breh lah keh-mah-DOO-rah, moo-EHS-treh-meh loh keh fweh.

Pregnancy Complications

Although officers are not medical personnel, they must ask key questions regarding pregnancy complications to help provide basic care until medical personnel arrive.

How many months/weeks pregnant are you?
¿Cuantos meses de embarazo tiene?
¿KWAHN-tohs MEH-sehs deh ehm-bah-RAH-soh tee-EH-neh?

What is your expected delivery date?
¿Cuál es la fecha del parto?
¿KWAHL ehs lah FEH-chah dehl PAHR-toh?

Have you had any other children?
¿Ha tenido otros hijos?
¿ah teh-NEE-doh oh-trohs EE-hohs?

Were there complications?
¿Hubo complicaciones?
¿OO-boh kohm-plee-kah-see-OH-nehs?

Have you had complications during this pregnancy?
¿Ha tenido complicaciones durante este embarazo?
¿ah teh-NEE-doh kohm-plee-kah-see-OH-nehs doo-RAHN-teh EHS-teh ehm-bah-RAH-soh?

Who is your doctor?
¿Quién es su doctor?
¿kee-EHN ehs soo dohk-TOHR?

How far apart are your contractions?
¿Cada cuánto son sus contracciones?
¿KAH-dah KWAHN-toh sohn soos kohn-trahk-see-OH-nehs?

Other than contractions, are you in any other pain?
¿A parte de las contracciones, tiene algún otro dolor?
¿ah PAHR-teh deh lahs kohn-trahk-see-OH-nehs, tee-EH-neh ahl-GOON OH-troh doh-LOHR?

Where?
¿Dónde?
¿DOHN-deh?

Delivering a Baby

What if the medical personnel have not arrived yet and you are on your own? Let's do this as basic as possible!

Medics are on their way.
Los paramédicos ya vienen.
lohs pah-rah-MEH-dee-kohs yah vee-EH-nehn.

I am going to help you deliver your baby.
Voy a ayudarle a dar a luz a su bebé.
voi ah ah-yoo-DAHR-leh ah dahr loos ah soo beh-BEH.

Open your legs.
Abra sus piernas.
AH-brah soos pee-EHR-nahs.

Push.
Empuje.
ehm-POO-heh.

Rest.
Descanse.
dehs-KAHN-seh.

Breathe.
Respire.
rehs-PEE-reh.

Helpful Phrases

When responding to incidents that involve the need for medical personnel, these phrases can help you offer comfort and aid to the victim:

Medical personnel are on their way.
El personal médico está en camino.
ehl pehr-soh-NAHL MEH-dee-koh ehs-TAH ehn kah-MEE-noh.

Try to stay calm.
Trate de calmarse.
TRAH-teh deh kahl-MAHR-seh.

I am not a doctor, but will help you until medical personnel arrive.
No soy doctor, pero voy a ayudarlo/la hasta que el personal médico llegue.
noh soi DOHK-tohr, PEH-roh voi ah ai-yoo-DAHR-loh/lah AHS-tah keh ehl pehr-SOH-nahl MEH-dee-koh YEH-geh.

Who can I contact for you?
¿A quién quiere que llame?
¿ah kee-EHN kee-EH-reh keh YAH-meh?

Name?
¿Nombre?
¿NOHM-breh?

Number?
¿Número?
¿NOO-meh-roh?

Chapter 5

Traffic Incidents

In This Chapter

- Getting the driver's information
- I'm giving you a ticket for …
- Handling traffic accidents
- When drivers have been drinking

This chapter focuses on traffic offenses, including obtaining license and registration information, accident investigations, and driving under the influence investigations.

Collecting Driver's Information

One of the first things to ask for during any incident, traffic related or not, is an ID. Ideally, the driver will have identification issued in the United States, but if he or she does not, obtain his or her out-of-country identification.

Do you have a license or identification?
¿Tiene licencia o identificación?
¿tee-EH-neh lee-SEHN-see-ah oh ee-dehn-tee-fee-kah-see-OHN?

You can ask for ID by simply saying, "¿Tiene ID?" (*¿tee-EH-neh ai-DEE?*) ID is commonly understood to mean "identification."

From the United States?
¿De los Estados Unidos?
¿deh lohs eh-STAH-dohs oo-NEE-dohs?

From which state?
¿De cuál estado?
¿deh KWAHL ehs-TAH-doh?

From which country?
¿De cuál país?
¿deh KWAHL pah-EES?

I would like to see it please.
Quiero verla, por favor.
kee-EH-roh VEHR-lah, pohr fah-VOHR.

Do you have car insurance?
¿Tiene seguro del carro?
¿tee-EH-neh seh-GOO-roh dehl KAHR-roh?

Do you have the registration?
¿Tiene el registro del carro?
¿tee-EH-neh ehl reh-HEE-stroh dehl KAHR-roh?

Keep it Simple

Sometimes subjects have been arrested using a different name than what they provide. The following question can help identify that name, providing additional criminal history on the subject.

Have you been arrested before in the United States?
¿Ha sido arrestado antes en los Estados Unidos?
¿ah SEE-doh ahr-rehs-TAH-doh AHN-tehs ehn lohs eh-STAH-dohs oo-NEE-dohs?

Giving a Ticket

This section provides a variety of reasons why someone would receive a citation, including moving violations, equipment violations, and paperwork infractions, and what you say during each.

I am going to give you a ticket.
Voy a darle una multa.
voi ah DAHR-leh OO-nah MOOL-tah.

Moving Violations

The following phrases help you explain why you stopped a person or otherwise tell them what they did wrong.

You were speeding.
Usted se excedió en su velocidad.
oo-STEHD seh ehx-seh-dee-OH ehn soo veh-loh-see-DAHD.

You did not stop for a red light.
Usted no paró cuando el semáforo estaba en rojo.
oo-STEHD noh pah-ROH KWAHN-doh ehl seh-MAH-foh-roh ehs-TAH-bah ehn ROH-hoh.

You did not stop for a stop sign.
Usted no paró en la señal de alto.
oo-STEHD noh pah-ROH ehn lah SEH-nyahl deh AHL-toh.

You failed to drive in one lane.
Usted no manejó en un solo carril.
oo-STEHD noh mah-neh-HOH eh oon SOH-loh kahr-REEL.

You made an unsafe lane change.
Usted cambió de carril peligrosamente.
oo-STEHD kahm-bee-OH deh KAHR-reel peh-lee-groh-sah-MEHN-teh.

You left the scene of an accident.
Usted abandonó el lugar del accidente.
oo-STEHD ah-bahn-doh-NOH ehl loo-GAHR dehl ahx-ee-DEHN-teh.

Equipment Violations

The following are some of the reasons someone
might receive an equipment violation.

Two headlights required
Se requieren dos luces delanteras
seh rehk-kee-EH-rohn dohs LOO-sehs deh-lahn-TEH-rahs

You have fictitious plates.
Tiene placas falsas.
tee-EH-neh PLAH-kahs FAHL-sahs.

You do not have a license plate.
No tiene placas.
noh tee-EH-neh PLAH-kahs.

Street Slang
To tell someone why they're receiving an equipment violation, simply point to the item and say, "*No tiene*" (*no tee-EH-neh*) or "you don't have."

Vehicle Parts

English	Spanish	Pronunciation
brake lights	luces de frenos	*LOO-sehs deh FREH-nohs*
bumper	defensa	*deh-FEHN-sah*
headlights	luces del frente	*LOO-sehs dehl FREHN-teh*
	Or:	
	luces delanteras	*LOO-sehs deh-lahn-TEH-rahs*
seat belt	cinturón/cinto de seguridad	*seen-too-ROHN/SEEN-toh deh seh-goo-ree-DAHD*
tail lights	luces traseras	*LOO-sehs trah-SEH-rahs*
turning lights	luces de giro/direccíonal	*LOO-sehs deh HEE-roh/ dee-rehk-see-oh-NAHL*
windshield	vidrio	*VEE-dree-oh*

Paperwork Infractions

Just like equipment violations, a multitude of paperwork infraction tickets can be written, especially if
you like working traffic and know your state codes.
These paperwork infractions will get you started.

**You failed to change your name on your driver's
license.**
Usted no ha cambiado el nombre en la licencia de
conducir.
*oo-STEHD noh ah kahm-bee-AH-doh ehl NOHM-
breh ehn lah lee-SEHN-see-ah deh kohn-doo-SEER.*

**You failed to change your address for your
driver's license.**
Usted no ha cambiado el domicilio en la licencia de
conducir.
*oo-STEHD noh ah kahm-bee-AH-doh ehl doh-mee-
SEE-lee-oh ehn lah lee-SEHN-see-ah deh kohn-doo-
SEER.*

**You failed to change your address for your
registration.**
Usted no ha cambiado el domicilio en el registro
del carro.
*oo-STEHD noh ah kahm-bee-AH-doh ehl doh-mee-
SEE-lee-oh ehn el reh-HEE-stroh dehl KAHR-roh.*

You failed to transfer the title within thirty days.
Usted no ha transferido el título del vehículo en
treinta días.
*oo-STEHD noh ah trahns-feh-REE-doh ehl TEE-too-
loh dehl veh-HEE-koo-loh ehn TREHN-tah DEE-ahs.*

You do not have a valid driver's license.
Usted no posee licencia de conducir válida.
*oo-STEHD noh poh-SEH-eh lee-SEHN-see-ah deh
kohn-doo-SEER VAH-lee-dah.*

You have a suspended driver's license.
Usted tiene una licencia de conducir suspendida.
*oo-STEHD tee-EH-neh OO-nah lee-SEHN-see-ah deh
kohn-doo-SEER soos-pehn-DEE-dah.*

You do not have mandatory insurance.
Usted no tiene el seguro obligatorio del vehículo.
*oo-STEHD noh tee-EH-neh ehl seh-GOO-roh oh-blee-
gah-TOH-ree-oh dehl veh-HEE-koo-loh.*

You have expired registration.
Usted tiene el registro vencido.
*oo-STEHD tee-EH-neh ehl reh-HEE-stroh vehn-SEE-
doh.*

**You can pay the ticket/fine, or you can go to
court.**
Usted puede pagar la multa, o puede ir a corte.
*oo-STEHD PWEH-deh pah-GAHR lah MOOL-tah,
oh PWEH-deh eer ah KOHR-teh.*

Traffic Accidents

Traffic accidents are one of the most common
calls officers respond to. This section helps you
gather basic information for accident investigations,
including hit-and-runs.

Gathering Basic Information

A lot of information needs to be gathered when investigating a traffic accident. Let's start with the basics.

Who was driving?
¿Quién estaba manejando?
¿kee-EHN ehs-TAH-bah mah-neh-HAHN-doh?

Which vehicle were you driving?
¿Qué carro estaba manejando?
¿keh KAHR-roh ehs-TAH-bah mah-neh-HAHN-doh?

Do you have a license or identification?
¿Tiene licencia o identificación?
¿tee-EH-neh lee-SEHN-see-ah oh ee-dehn-tee-fee-kah-see-OHN?

I would like to see it, please.
Quiero verla, por favor.
kee-EH-roh VEHR-lah, pohr fah-VOHR.

Are there witnesses?
¿Hay testigos?
¿ai tehs-TEE-gohs?

If yes:

Who?
¿Quién?
¿kee-EHN?

Which direction were you coming from?
¿De qué dirección venía?
¿deh KEH dee-rehk-see-OHN veh-NEE-ah?

Which lane?
¿En cuál carril?
¿ehn KWAHL kahr-REEL?

Your speed?
¿Su velocidad?
¿soo veh-loh-see-DAHD?

Where did the other car come from?
¿De dónde venía el otro carro?
¿deh DOHN-deh veh-NEE-ah ehl OH-troh KAHR-roh?

Which lane was it in?
¿En cuál carril venía?
¿ehn KWAHL kahr-REEL veh-NEE-ah?

Were there passengers?
¿Había pasajeros?
¿ah-BEE-ah pah-sah-HEH-rohs?

Where are they?
¿Dónde están?
¿DOHN-deh ehs-TAHN?

What color was the traffic light?
¿De qué color estaba el semáforo?
¿deh KEH koh-LOHR eh-STAH-bah ehl seh-MAH-foh-roh?

Did you see the stop sign?
¿Vio la señal de alto?
¿vee-OH lah seh-NYAHL deh AHL-toh?

Were you wearing your seat belt?
¿Tenía puesto su cinturón/cinto de seguridad?
*¿teh-NEE-ah poo-EHS-toh soo seen-too-ROHN/SEEN-
toh deh seh-goo-ree-DAHD?*

When Someone Is Injured

It is important to find out if someone feels they
are injured from their car accident. If you don't see
any visible injuries, you have to ask them. It would
then also be important to ask where the injury is for
both medical personnel, if responding, and for your
report.

Are you injured?
¿Está lastimado/a?
¿ehs-TAH lah-stee-MAH-doh/dah?

Do you need medical attention? Yes or no?
¿Necesita atención médica? ¿Sí o no?
*¿neh-seh-SEE-tah ah-tehn-see-OHN MEH-dee-kah?
¿see oh noh?*

Where are you hurt?
¿Adónde está golpeado?
¿ah-DOHN-deh ehs-TAH gohl-peh-AH-doh?

Hit-and-Runs

When you respond to a hit-and-run call, here's
some questions you can ask.

Did the other vehicle leave?
¿El otro vehículo se fue?
¿ehl OH-troh veh-HEE-koo-loh seh fweh?

What type was it?
¿Qué tipo era?
¿KEH TEE-poh EH-rah?

Types of Vehicles

English	Spanish	Pronunciation
bike	bicicleta	*bee-see-KLEH-tah*
car	carro	*KAHR-roh*
	coche	*KOH-cheh*
	auto	*AH-oo-toh*
extended cab	doble cabina	*DOH-bleh kah-BEE-nah*
motorcycle	moto	*MOH-toh*
pick-up truck	camión	*kah-mee-OHN*
van	camioneta	*kah-mee-oh-NEH-tah*
bus	bus/guagua	*boos/goo-AH-wah*
taxi	taxi	*TAHK-see*
trailer	el tráiler/la traila	*ehl TRAH-ee-lehr/ lah TRAH-ee-lah*

Street Slang *Camioneta (kah-mee-oh-NEH-tah) can also refer to a pick-up truck, so be sure to verify what type of vehicle they're referring to. The word van (bahn) is often used for van as well, and troca (TROH-kah) for a pick-up truck.*

What class/brand was it?
¿Qué clase era?
¿keh KLAH-seh EH-rah?

The year?
¿El año?
¿ehl AH-nyoh?

Was it new or old?
¿Era nuevo o viejo?
¿EH-rah noo-EH-voh oh vee-EH-hoh?

What color was it?
¿Qué color era?
¿KEH koh-LOHR EH-rah?

Good or badly painted?
¿Bien o mal pintado?
¿bee-EHN o mahl peen-TAH-doh?

Rusty?
¿Oxidado?
¿ohx-ee-DAH-doh?

With stickers?
¿Con calcomanías?
¿kohn kahl-koh-mah-NEE-ahs?

Two or four doors?
¿Dos o cuatro puertas?
¿dohs o KWAH-troh poo-EHR-tahs?

Numbers/letters of the license plate?
¿Números/letras de la placa?
¿NOO-meh-rohs/LEH-trahs deh lah PLAH-kah?

State?
¿Estado?
¿ehs-TAH-doh?

Road Distress Calls

This section lists some key phrases you can use to assist stranded motorists.

Do you need a tow truck?
¿Necesita una grúa?
¿neh-seh-SEE-tah OO-nah GROO-ah?

Do you need to call someone?
¿Necesita llamar a alguien?
¿neh-seh-SEE-tah yah-MAHR ah AHL-gee-ehn?

Do you have a spare tire?
¿Tiene una rueda/llanta de auxilio?
¿tee-EH-neh OO-nah roo-EH-dah/YAHN-tah deh aux-EE-lee-oh?

Would you like me to help you change your tire?
¿Necesita que lo/la ayude a cambiar su rueda/llanta?
¿neh-seh-SEE-tah keh loh/lah ah-YOO-deh ah kahm-bee-AHR soo roo-EH-dah/YAHN-tah?

Would you like a ride?
¿Quiere que lo/la lleve a alguna parte?
¿kee-EH-reh keh loh/lah YEH-veh ah ahl-GOO-nah PAHR-teh?

Do you want me to call you a taxi?
¿Quiere que llame un taxi?
¿kee-EH-reh keh YAH-meh oon TAHK-see?

Driving Under the Influence

The following field sobriety tests and line of questioning are not meant to replace your department's forms or protocol. They're intended to help you obtain pertinent information for a DUI investigation.

Field Sobriety Tests

Most states use at least four field sobriety tests (FSTs)—the walk and turn, finger count, finger to nose, and one leg stand, as well as a horizontal gaze nystagmus (HGN) test. If you have a portable breath test (PBT), it makes it even easier. In this section, we go through the four FSTs, the HGN test, and a PBT test.

Have you been drinking?
¿Ha estado tomando?
¿ah ehs-TAH-doh toh-MAHN-doh?

Do you have any physical disabilities? Yes or no?
¿Usted tiene alguna discapacidad física? ¿Sí o no?
¿oo-STEHD tee-EH-neh ahl-GOO-nah dees-kah-pah-see-DAHD FEE-see-kah? ¿see oh noh?

We are going to perform some tests, okay?
Vamos a hacer unos exámenes, ¿de acuerdo?
VAH-mohs ah ah-SEHR OO-nohs ehx-AH-meh-nehs,
¿deh ah-KWEHR-doh?

Portable breathalyzer test (PBT):

Blow into this tube until I tell you to stop.
Sople en este tubo hasta que le diga que pare.
SOH-pleh ehn EHS-teh TOO-boh AHS-tah keh leh
DEE-gah keh PAH-reh.

One leg stand:

Stand with your feet together ...
Párese con sus pies juntos ...
PAH-reh-seh kohn soos PEE-ehs HOON-tohs ...

... arms down at your side, like this.
... sus brazos en los lados, así.
... soos BRAH-sohs ehn lohs LAH-dohs, ah-SEE.

Do you understand? Yes or no.
¿Entiende? Sí o no
¿ehn-tee-EHN-deh? see oh no.

Do it please.
Hágalo por favor.
AH-gah-loh pohr fah-VOHR.

Maintain that position.
Mantenga esta posición.
mahn-TEHN-gah EHS-tah poh-see-see-OHN.

Raise one leg straight out about six inches off the ground.
Levante una pierna unas seis pulgadas del suelo.
leh-VAHN-teh OO-nah pee-EHR-nah OO-nahs SEH-ehs pool-GAH-dahs dehl SWEH-loh.

Keep your leg straight.
Mantenga su pierna estirada.
mahn-TEHN-gah soo pee-EHR-nah ehs-tee-RAH-dah.

Hold that position, look at your foot, and count to twenty out loud.
Mantenga esta posición, mire el pie, y cuente hasta veinte en voz alta.
mahn-TEHN-gah EHS-tah poh-see-see-OHN, MEE-reh ehl pee-EH, ee KWEHN-teh AHS-tah VEHN-teh ehn vohs AHL-tah.

Finger count:

Stand with your feet together.
Párese con sus pies juntos.
PAH-reh-seh kohn soos pee-EHS HOON-tohs.

Count out loud "one, two, three, four, four, three, two, one" while touching each finger with your thumb, like this.
Cuente en voz alta "uno, dos, tres, cuatro, cuatro, tres, dos, uno" mientras toca cada dedo con su dedo gordo, así.
KWEHN-teh ehn vohs AHL-tah "OO-noh, dohs, trehs, KWAH-troh, KWAH-troh, trehs, dohs, OO-noh" mee-EHN-trahs TOH-kah KAH-dah DEH-doh kohn soo DEH-doh GOHR-doh, ah-SEE.

Finger to nose:

Stand with your feet together ...
Párese con sus pies juntos ...
PAH-reh-seh kohn soos pee-EHS HOON-tohs ...

... arms down at your side, like this.
... sus brazos en los lados, así.
... soos BRAH-sohs ehn lohs LAH-dohs, ah-SEE.

Now, close your eyes and tilt your head back.
Ahora, cierre sus ojos y ponga su cabeza hacia atrás.
ah-OH-rah, see-EHR-reh soos OH-hohs ee POHN-gah soo kah-BEH-sah ah-TRAHS.

Good. Now, touch your nose with one finger.
Bien. Ahora, toque la punta de su nariz con la punta de su dedo.
bee-EHN. ah-OH-rah, TOH-keh lah POON-tah deh soo nah-REES kohn lah POON-tah deh soo DEH-doh.

Horizontal gaze nystagmus:

Take off your glasses.
Quítese sus lentes.
KEE-teh-seh soos LEHN-tehs.

Are you wearing contact lenses?
¿Lleva usted lentes de contacto?
¿YEH-vah oo-STEHD LEHN-tehs deh kohn-TAHK-toh?

Keep your head still. Follow the point of this pen/this light with your eyes.

Mantenga la cabeza inmóvil. Siga la punta de este bolígrafo/esta luz con sus ojos.

mahn-TEHN-gah lah kah-BEH-sah een-MOH-veel.
SEE-gah lah POON-tah de EHS-teh boh-LEE-grah-foh/EHS-tah loos kohn soos OH-hohs.

Alcohol Influence Report

The following questions will help you fill out your Alcohol Influence Report and are used to obtain some of the most important information for this investigation.

Were you operating the vehicle? Yes or no?

¿Estaba manejando el vehículo? ¿Sí o no?

¿ehs-TAH-bah mah-neh-HAHN-doh ehl veh-HEE-koo-loh? ¿see oh noh?

Where were you going?

¿Para dónde iba?

¿PAH-rah DOHN-deh EE-bah?

From where did you start?

¿De dónde salió?

¿deh DOHN-deh sah-lee-OH?

At what time did you leave?

¿A qué hora se fue?

¿ah KEH OH-rah seh fweh?

What time is it now?

¿Qué hora es ahora?

¿KEH OH-rah ehs ah-OH-rah?

What is the date today?
¿Cuál es la fecha de hoy?
¿KWAHL ehs lah FEH-chah deh oi?

What day of the week is it?
¿Qué día de la semana es hoy?
¿KEH DEE-ah deh lah seh-MAH-nah ehs oi?

What have you been drinking?
¿Qué ha estado tomando?
¿KEH ah ehs-TAH-doh toh-MAHN-doh?

How much did you drink?
¿Cuánto ha tomado?
¿KWAHN-toh ah toh-MAH-doh?

Where were you drinking?
¿Adónde estaba tomando?
¿ah-DOHN-deh ehs-TAH-bah toh-MAHN-doh?

What time did you start drinking?
¿A qué hora empezó a tomar?
¿ah KEH OH-rah ehm-peh-SOH a toh-MAHR?

What time did you stop drinking?
¿A qué hora paró de tomar?
¿ah KEH OH-rah pah-ROH deh toh-MAHR?

Did you have an accident? Yes or no?
¿Tuvo un accidente? ¿Sí o no?
¿TOO-voh oon ahx-ee-DEHN-teh? ¿see oh noh?

If yes:

Where?
¿Adónde?
¿ah-DOHN-deh?

What time did the accident occur?
¿A qué hora ocurrió el accidente?
¿ah KEH OH-rah oh-koo-ree-OH ehl ahx-ee-DEHN-teh?

A vehicle accident is often referred to as a *choque* (*CHOH-keh*). An *accidente* can refer to any type of accident, not just a vehicle accident.

At what location were you stopped?
¿Dónde fue que la policía lo paró?
¿DOHN-deh fweh keh lah poh-lee-SEE-ah loh pah-ROH?

Are you ill? Yes or no?
¿Está enfermo? ¿Sí o no?
¿ehs-TAH ehn-FEHR-moh? ¿see oh noh?

Have you taken any medication in the past twenty-four hours? Yes or no?
¿Ha tomado algún medicamento en las últimas veinticuatro horas? ¿Sí o no?
¿ah toh-MAH-doh ahl-GOON meh-dee-kah-MEHN-toh ehn lahs OOL-tee-mahs vehn-tee-KWAH-troh OH-rahs? ¿see oh noh?

Do you have diabetes? Yes or no?
¿Usted tiene diabetes? ¿Sí o no?
¿oo-STEHD tee-EH-neh dee-ah-BEH-tehs? ¿see oh noh?

Blood Draw

Some states are transitioning to mandatory blood draws over using the breathalyzer tests. This will make your translating very easy.

We are going to take a sample of your blood; will you comply?
Vamos a tomar una muestra de su sangre; ¿está de acuerdo?
VAH-mohs ah toh-MAHR OO-nah moo-EHS-trah deh soo SAHN-greh; ¿ehs-TAH deh ah-KWEHR-doh?

Helpful Phrases

This section lists some words and phrases that will be useful when you're confronted with a traffic investigation of any kind.

Get out of the car, please.
Salga del carro, por favor.
SAHL-gah dehl KAHR-roh, pohr fah-VOHR.

You are arrested/under arrest.
Está arrestado.
ehs-TAH ahr-rehs-TAH-doh.

Sign here.
Firme aquí.
FEER-meh ah-KEE.

Can I search your car?
¿Puedo registrar su carro?
¿PWEH-doh reh-hee-STRAHR soo KAHR-roh?

Do you want to leave your car here, or do you want it towed?

¿Quiere dejar su carro aquí, o quiere que se lo lleve la grúa?

¿kee-EH-reh deh-HAHR soo KAHR-roh ah-KEE, oh kee-EH-reh keh seh loh YEH-vah lah GROO-ah?

Chapter 6

Violent Crimes

In This Chapter

- Assaults and domestic violence
- Were you robbed?
- Were you raped?
- Dealing with kidnappings
- Shootings and homicides

Violent crime investigations can be stressful, confusing situations for first responders. The questions in this chapter are designed to help you determine what crime occurred and elicit information needed for a basic report.

General Assault

A general assault occurs when someone known (of no relation) or unknown to the victim attempts to cause or causes injury with or without the use of a weapon. You'll need to get information from both the victim and the suspect.

Questions for Victims

You need some basic information from the victim to assist in your investigation. The following questions will get you started.

Did someone hit you?
¿Alguien te pegó?
¿AHL-gee-ehn teh peh-GOH?

Who hit you?
¿Quién te pegó?
¿kee-EHN teh peh-GOH?

How were you hit?
¿Cómo te pegó?
¿KOH-moh teh peh-GOH?

With an open hand or a closed hand?
¿Con mano abierta o cerrada?
¿kohn MAH-noh ah-bee-EHR-tah oh seh-RAH-dah?

Right or left hand?
¿Mano derecha o izquierda?
¿MAH-noh deh-REH-chah oh ees-kee-EHR-dah?

Did he/she use a weapon?
¿Usó un arma?
¿oo-SOH oon AHR-mah?

What type?
¿Qué tipo?
¿KEH TEE-poh?

Assault Weapons

English	Spanish	Pronunciation
bat	bate	*BAH-teh*
brick	ladrillo	*lah-DREE-yoh*
household knife	cuchillo	*koo-CHEE-yoh*
Slang:	fila	*FEE-lah*
hunting knife (*slang*)	filero	*fee-LEH-roh*
pipe	pipa	*PEE-pah*
pocket knife	navaja	*nah-VAH-hah*
stick	palo	*PAH-loh*

How many times were you hit?
¿Cuántas veces te pegó?
¿KWAHN-tahs VEH-sehs teh PEH-goh?

Where were you hit? Show me.
¿Dónde te pegó? Enséñame.
¿DOHN-deh teh peh-GOH? ehn-SEH-nyah-meh.

Do you have injuries?
¿Tienes heridas?
¿tee-EH-nehs eh-REE-dahs?

Do you have bruises?
¿Tiene moretones/morados?
¿tee-EH-nehs moh-reh-TOH-nehs/moh-RAH-dohs?

Injuries

English	Spanish	Pronunciation
bump	chichón/ bulto	*chee-CHOHN/* *BOOL-toh*
cut	corte/ cortadura	*KOHR-teh/* *kohr-tah-DOO-rah*
laceration	corte profundo	*KOHR-teh* *proh-FOON-do*
scrape, "raspberry"	raspadura	*rahs-pah-DOO-rah*
scratch	arañazo	*ah-rah-NYAH-soh*
	rasguño	*rahs-GOO-nyoh*
swelling	hinchazón	*een-chah-SOHN*

Are you in pain?
¿Tiene dolor?
¿tee-EH-neh doh-LOHR?

How many people attacked you?
¿Cuánta gente lo/la atacó?
¿KWAHN-tah HEHN-teh loh/lah ah-tah-KOH?

Do you know him/her/them?
¿Lo/la/los/las conoce?
¿loh/lah/lohs/lahs koh-NOH-seh?

Are they still here?
¿Están todavia aquí?
¿ehs-TAHN toh-dah-VEE-ah ah-KEE?

Show me who it was.
Muéstreme quien fue.
moo-EHS-streh-meh kee-EHN fweh.

Questions for Suspects

If you are fortunate enough to catch the suspect(s) or the suspect(s) is still at the scene, you need to obtain both sides of the story.

Do you know the victim?
¿Conoce usted a la víctima?
¿koh-NOH-seh oo-STEHD ah lah VEEK-tee-mah?

Stop Sign

Whenever asking a suspect questions, be cautious of Miranda issues. Miranda still applies even if you're not a proficient Spanish speaker.

Did you hit him/her?
¿Le pegó?
¿leh peh-GOH?

Did you hit him/her with your hand/fist/foot?
¿Le pegó con su mano/puño/pie?
¿leh peh-GOH kohn soo MAH-noh/POO-nyoh/pee-EH?

Did you intend to injure him/her?
¿Su intención fue lastimarlo/a?
¿soo een-tehn-see-OHN fweh lahs-tee-MAHR-loh/lah?

What type of weapon did you use?
¿Qué tipo de arma usó?
¿KEH TEE-poh deh AHR-mah oo-SOH?

Tell me where the weapon is.
Dígame dónde está el arma.
DEE-gah-meh DOHN-deh ehs-TAH ehl AHR-mah.

Domestic Violence

In most states, domestic violence crimes and subsequent reports require certain information, especially to establish a relationship between the suspect and the victim. The following questions are designed to establish the extent of the relationship and obtain specific information about the crimes.

Stop fighting.
Dejen de pelear.
DEH-hehn deh peh-leh-AHR.

Stop yelling.
Dejen de gritar.
DEH-hehn de gree-TAHR.

I need to know what happened.
Necesito saber qué pasó.
neh-seh-SEE-toh sah-BEHR KEH pah-SOH.

Questions for Victims

The following questions help you establish the relationship and let you know if you have a domestic violence situation or not.

Is he/she a blood relative?
¿Es pariente?
¿ehs pah-ree-EHN-teh?

Currently married:

Are you married?
¿Están casados?
¿ehs-TAHN kah-SAH-dohs?

How long have you been married?
¿Por cuánto tiempo han estado casados?
*¿pohr KWAHN-toh tee-EHM-poh ahn ehs-TAH-doh
kah-SAH-dohs?*

Who lives here?
¿Quién vive aquí?
¿kee-EHN VEE-veh ah-KEE?

Street Slang If someone is having an affair, the words *sancha* (*SAHN-chah*) or *sancho* (*SAHN-choh*) refer to the "other woman" or "other man," respectively.

Previously married:

Were you married?
¿Estaban casados?
¿ehs-TAH-bahn kah-SAH-dohs?

How long were you married?
¿Por cuánto tiempo estuvieron casados?
*¿pohr KWAHN-toh tee-EHM-poh ehs-too-vee-EH-
rohn kah-SAH-dohs?*

How long have you been divorced?
¿Por cuánto tiempo han estado divorciados?
¿pohr KWAHN-toh tee-EHM-poh ahn ehs-TAH-doh
dee-vohr-see-AH-dohs?

Living together:

Do you live together?
¿Viven juntos?
¿VEE-vehn HOON-tohs?

How long have you lived together?
¿Por cuánto tiempo han vivido juntos?
¿pohr KWAHN-toh tee-EHM-poh ahn vee-VEE-doh
HOON-tohs?

Previously living together:

Did you live together?
¿Vivían juntos?
¿vee-VEE-ahn HOON-tohs?

How long did you live together?
¿Por cuánto tiempo vivieron juntos?
¿pohr KWAHN-toh tee-EHM-poh ahn vee-vee-EH-
rohn HOON-tohs?

How long have you lived separately?
¿Por cuánto tiempo viven separados?
¿pohr KWAHN-toh tee-EHM-poh VEE-vehn seh-pah-
RAH-dohs?

Children in common:

Do you have children together?
¿Tienen niños juntos?
¿tee-EH-nehn NEE-nyohs HOON-tohs?

How many?
¿Cuántos?
¿KWAHN-tohs?

How old are the children?
¿Cuántos años tienen los niños?
¿KWAHN-tohs AH-nyohs tee-EH-nehn lohs NEE-nyohs?

How old is your son/daughter?
¿Cuántos años tiene su niño/niña?
¿KWAHN-tohs AH-nyohs tee-EH-neh soo NEE-nyoh/ NEE-nyah?

Questions for Suspects

As with all investigations, when possible, it's important to get both sides of the story. Obtaining an entire story would be ideal, but with limited Spanish your investigation is limited. The following questions help determine the suspect's state of mind for prosecution.

Did you assault him/her?
¿Usted le pegó?
¿oo-STEHD leh peh-GOH?

Did you know the children were present?
¿Sabía que los niños estaban presentes?
¿sah-BEE-ah keh lohs NEE-nyohs ehs-TAH-bahn preh-SEHN-tehs?

Robbery

When something is stolen from a victim by force or with the use or threatened use of a weapon, this is considered a robbery. The following questions help you determine what happened.

Questions for Victims

If possible, get the victim's story first.

Did you see who did this?
¿Vio quien hizo esto?
¿vee-OH kee-EHN EE-soh EHS-toh?

Can you describe him/her?
¿Puede describirlo/la?
¿PWEH-deh dehs-kree-BEER-loh/lah?

How many suspects were there?
¿Cuántos sospechosos había?
¿KWAHN-tohs sohs-peh-CHOH-sohs ah-BEE-ah?

What was stolen?
¿Qué han robado?
¿KEH ahn roh-BAH-doh?

Did they have weapons?
¿Tenían armas?
¿teh-NEE-ahn AHR-mahs?

What type?
¿Qué tipo?
¿KEH TEE-poh?

Keep it Simple   If someone is giving a long-winded response to your questions, use the phrase *"Dígame sí o no"* (*DEE-gah-meh see oh noh;* "tell me yes or no") to shorten his or her response to a closed-ended question.

Did they point the gun at you?
¿Lo/la apuntaron con un arma?
¿loh/lah ah-poon-TAH-rohn kohn oon AHR-mah?

More or less, at what time did this occur?
¿Más o menos, a que hora ocurrió?
¿MAHS oh MEH-nohs, ah keh OH-rah oh-koo-ree-OH?

Where did it occur?
¿Dónde ocurrió?
¿DOHN-deh oh-koo-ree-OH?

Did they leave on foot or in a vehicle?
¿Se fueron a pie o en un vehículo?
¿seh FWEH-rohn ah pee-EH oh eh oon veh-HEE-koo-loh?

When?
¿Cuándo?
¿KWAHN-doh?

Which direction?
¿En qué dirección?
¿ehn KEH dee-rehk-see-OHN?

Questions for Suspects

Suspects admit to amazing things. Do not hesitate to determine whether the suspect will confess to the crime. You can do this with just a few questions.

Did you rob someone?
¿Usted robó a alguien?
¿oo-STEHD roh-BOH ah AHL-gee-ehn?

Did you steal this item?
¿Usted robó este objeto?
¿oo-STEHD roh-BOH EHS-teh ohb-HEH-toh?

Did you use force?
¿Lo hizo por la fuerza?
¿loh EE-soh pohr lah foo-EHR-sah?

Did you use a weapon?
¿Usó un arma?
¿oo-SOH oon AHR-mah?

Sexual Assault

Sexual assaults are one of the most sensitive situations law enforcement officers encounter. After making sure the potential victim is safe from further harm, it's recommended to have a fluent Spanish speaker, if possible, assume the investigation so as not to potentially offend the victim with unintentional comments.

Questions for Victims

Although it's difficult, asking the victim these questions up front enables you to establish the parameters of the crime.

Were you raped?
¿Fue violada/o?
¿fweh vee-oh-LAH-dah/doh?

Do you know the suspect?
¿Conoce al sospechoso?
¿koh-NOH-seh ahl sohs-peh-CHOH-soh?

Is he here right now?
¿Está él aquí en este momento?
¿ehs-TAH EHL ah-KEE ehn EHS-teh moh-MEHN-toh?

Did he penetrate you?
¿Él lo/la penetró?
¿EHL loh/lah peh-neh-TROH?

Where?
¿Dónde?
¿DOHN-deh?

With his penis?
¿Con su pene?
¿kohn soo PEH-neh?

Fingers?
¿Dedos?
¿DEH-dohs?

Did he penetrate you with anything else?
¿Lo/la penetró con algo más?
¿*loh/lah peh-neh-TROH kohn AHL-goh MAHS?*

Sexual References

English	Spanish	Pronunciation
anus	ano	*AH-noh*
Slang:	cola	*KOH-lah*
	culo	*KOO-loh*
	fundillo	*foon-DEE-yoh*
breast	pecho	*PEH-choh*
Slang:	chichas	*CHEE-chahs*
	tetas	*TEH-tahs*
buttocks	glúteos	*GLOO-teh-ohs*
Slang:	nalgas	*NAHL-gahs*
ejaculate	eyacular	*eh-yah-koo-LAHR*
Slang:	correrse	*kohr-REHR-seh*
	venirse	*veh-NEER-seh*
penis	pene	*PEH-neh*
semen	semen	*SEH-mehn*
Slang:	arroz con leche	*ahr-ROHS kohn LEH-cheh*
	leche	*LEH-cheh*
	orchata	*ohr-CHAH-tah*
sex	tener relaciones sexuales	*teh-NEHR reh-lah-see-OHN-ehs sehx-oo-AHL-ehs*
Slang:	coger	*koh-HEHR*
	costear	*kohs-TEH-ahr*
	culear	*koo-leh-AHR*

English	Spanish	Pronunciation
testicles	testículos	*tehs-TEE-koo-lohs*
Slang:	cojones	*koh-HOHN-ehs*
	huevos	*oo-EH-vohs*
vagina	vagina	*vah-HEE-nah*
Slang:	bacalao	*bah-kah-LAH-oh*
	panocha	*pah-NOH-chah*
	vulva	*VOOL-vah*

When did this occur?
¿Cuándo ocurrió?
¿KWAHN-doh oh-koo-ree-OH?

Where did this occur?
¿Dónde ocurrió?
¿DOHN-deh oh-koo-ree-OH?

Have you showered?
¿Se ha bañado?
¿seh ah bah-NYAH-doh?

Are those the clothes you were wearing at the time?
¿Ésta es la ropa que tenía puesta cuando pasó?
¿EHS-tah ehs lah ROH-pah keh teh-NEE-ah PWEHS-tah KWAHN-doh pah-SOH?

Where are the clothes you were wearing at the time?
¿Dónde esta la ropa que tenía puesta cuando pasó?
¿DOHN-deh EHS-tah lah ROH-pah keh teh-NEE-ah PWEHS-tah KWAHN-doh pah-SOH?

Will you get an exam by a nurse?
¿Va a examinarse con una enfermera?
¿vah ah ehx-ah-mee-NAHR-seh kohn OO-nah ehn-fehr-MEH-rah?

Questions for Suspects

With suspects in a sexual assault investigation, ideally, a fluent Spanish speaker will be available to interview him/her. If not, you need to establish a few things with the suspect.

Did you rape him/her?
¿Lo/la violó?
¿loh/lah vee-oh-LOH?

Did he/she say "no"?
¿Él/ella dijo "no"?
¿EHL/eyah DEE-hoh "noh"?

Did you know his/her age?
¿Sabe usted cuántos años tiene él/ella?
¿SAH-beh oo-STEHD KWAHN-tohs AH-nyohs tee-EH-neh EHL/eyah?

At what location did you rape him/her?
¿En dónde estaban cuando lo/la violó?
¿ehn DOHN-deh ehs-TAH-bahn KWAHN-doh loh/lah vee-oh-LOH?

In which room?
¿En qué cuarto?
¿ehn KEH KWAHR-toh?

Kidnapping

This section addresses the crime of kidnapping (not related to human smuggling). Ideally, the questions will enable you to obtain enough information to identify the location of the crime.

Questions for Victims

Use these questions if you have a victim to interview, rather than a witness calling in a kidnapping with the victim missing.

Were you kidnapped?
¿Fue secuestrado?
¿fweh seh-kweh-STRAH-doh?

Where were you taken from?
¿De dónde se lo/la llevaron?
¿deh DOHN-deh seh loh/lah yeh-VAH-rohn?

When?
¿Cuándo?
¿KWAHN-doh?

How many days ago?
¿Hace cuántos días?
¿AH-seh KWAHN-tohs DEE-ahs?

Do you know your kidnapper?
¿Sabe quién es el secuestrador?
¿SAH-beh kee-EHN ehs ehl seh-kweh-strah-DOHR?

Where were you kept?
¿Dónde lo/la tenían escondido/a?
¿DOHN-deh loh/lah teh-NEE-ahn ehs-kohn-DEE-doh/dah?

Can you show me where?
¿Me puede mostrar dónde?
¿meh PWEH-deh moh-STRAHR DOHN-deh?

Questions for Suspects

You need to establish a few important facts with the suspect.

Did you have permission to take him/her?
¿Tenía permiso de llevárselo/la?
¿teh-NEE-ah pehr-MEE-soh deh yeh-VAHR-seh-loh/lah?

Who gave you permission?
¿Quién le dio permiso?
¿kee-EHN leh DEE-oh pehr-MEE-soh?

Where did you take him/her from?
¿Dónde lo/la llevó?
¿DOHN-deh loh/lah yeh-VOH?

Have you kidnapped anyone else?
¿Ha secuestrado a alguien más?
¿ah seh-kweh-STRAH-doh ah AHL-gee-ehn mahs?

Is he/she alive?
¿Está vivo/a?
¿ehs-TAH VEE-voh/vah?

Where is he/she?
¿Dónde está?
¿DOHN-deh ehs-TAH?

Did you provide him/her with food and water?
¿Usted le dio comida y agua?
¿oo-STEHD leh DEE-oh koh-MEE-dah ee AH-gwah?

Shooting

When a shooting occurs, it's important to obtain
certain information quickly to apprehend the suspect and/or to conduct your investigation safely.

Questions for Victims

With limited Spanish, you can only attempt to
obtain the basic information to either look for the
suspects and/or determine whether you're safe
where you're conducting the investigation.

Where are you shot?
¿Dónde está herido/a?
¿DOHN-deh ehs-TAH eh-REE-doh/dah?

Is anyone else shot?
¿Hay alguien más herido?
¿ai AHL-gee-ehn MAHS eh-REE-doh?

How many people are shot?
¿Cuánta gente ha sido herida?
¿KWAHN-tah HEHN-teh ah SEE-doh eh-REE-dah?

Was it a handgun, rifle, or shotgun?
¿Fue un arma de mano, un rifle, o una escopeta?
¿fweh oon AHR-mah deh MAH-noh, oon REE-fleh, oh OO-nah ehs-koh-PEH-tah?

Did you see the suspects?
¿Vio a los sospechosos?
¿VEE-oh ah lohs sohs-peh-CHOH-sohs?

How long ago did you last see the suspects?
¿Cuándo fue la última vez que vio a los sospechosos?
¿KWAHN-doh fweh lah OOL-tee-mah vehs keh VEE-oh ah lohs sohs-peh-CHOH-sohs?

Were they in a vehicle or on foot?
¿Andaban en un vehículo o a pie?
¿ahn-DAH-bahn ehn oon veh-HEE-koo-loh oh ah pee-EH?

Do you have a gun?
¿Tiene usted un arma?
¿tee-EH-neh oo-STEHD oon AHR-mah?

Did you shoot back?
¿Usted disparó después?
¿oo-STEHD dees-pah-ROH dehs-PWEHS?

Ballistic Weapons

English	Spanish	Pronunciation
AK-47/submachine gun	subfusil	*soob-foo-SEEL*
Slang:	cuerno de chivo	*KWEHR-noh deh CHEE-voh*
automatic rifle	automático/a	*ah-oo-toh-MAH-tee-koh/kah*
handgun/pistol	pistola	*pees-TOH-lah*
Slang:	cuete	*koo-EH-teh*
	fierro	*fee-EHR-roh*
	fuca	*FOO-kah*
	fusca	*FOOS-kah*
machine gun	ametralladora	*ah-meh-trah-yah-DOH-rah*
	metralleta	*meh-trah-YEH-tah*
rifle	rifle/fusil	*REE-fleh*
semiautomatic	semiautomática	*seh-mee-ah-oo-toh-MAH-tee-kah*
Slang:	cuadrada	*kwah-DRAH-dah*
shotgun	escopeta	*ehs-koh-PEH-tah*

Questions for Suspects

Remember Miranda warnings when appropriate because the following questions will be incriminating if answered.

Did you intentionally shoot him/her?
¿Le disparó a propósito?
¿leh dees-pah-ROH ah proh-POH-see-toh?

Where were you aiming at?
¿A dónde le apuntó?
¿ah DOHN-deh leh ah-poon-TOH?

Did he/she have a weapon at the time you shot him/her?
¿Tenía él/ella un arma cuando usted le disparó?
¿teh-NEE-ah EHL/eyah oon AHR-mah KWAHN-doh oo-STEHD leh dees-pah-ROH?

Where is the weapon you used?
¿Dónde está el arma que usó?
¿DOHN-deh ehs-TAH ehl AHR-mah keh oo-SOH?

Do you have any other weapons at any other locations?
¿Tiene usted otra arma en algún otro lugar?
¿tee-EH-neh oo-STEHD OH-trah AHR-mah ehn ahl-GOON OH-troh loo-GAHR?

Homicide

When responding to a homicide, it's pertinent to determine if there were witnesses and, if so, to obtain their stories. The following questions help you get the information you need to put the pieces together.

Questions for Witnesses

There's no victim to interview in a homicide investigation, so you'll question witnesses.

Did anyone see anything?
¿Alguien vio algo?
¿AHL-gee-ehn vee-OH AHL-goh?

Does anyone know the victim?
¿Alguien conoce a la víctima?
¿AHL-gee-ehn koh-NOH-seh ah lah VEEK-tee-mah?

Does anyone know the victim's name?
¿Hay alguien que sepa el nombre de la víctima?
¿ai AHL-gee-ehn keh SEH-pah ehl NOHM-breh deh lah VEEK-tee-mah?

What is it?
¿Cuál es?
¿koo-AHL ehs?

Do you know anyone who wanted to harm the victim?
¿Sabe de alguien que quería lastimar a la víctima?
¿SAH-beh deh AHL-gee-ehn keh keh-REE-ah lahs-tee-MAHR ah lah VEEK-tee-mah?

Are you related to the victim?
¿Es usted pariente de la víctima?
¿ehs oo-STEHD pah-ree-EHN-teh deh lah VEEK-tee-mah?

Where did the victim live?
¿Dónde vivía la víctima?
¿DOHN-deh vee-VEE-ah lah VEEK-tee-mah?

When was the victim injured?
¿Dónde fue herida la víctima?
¿DOHN-deh fweh eh-REE-dah lah VEEK-tee-mah?

Question for Suspects

This interview will be very incriminating. Be careful when proceeding to talk to a homicide suspect.

Did you know the victim?
¿Conocía a la víctima?
¿koh-noh-SEE-ah ah lah VEEK-tee-mah?

Did you intentionally kill him/her?
¿Lo/la mató intencionalmente?
¿loh/lah mah-TOH een-tehn-see-oh-nahl-MEHN-teh?

Did you know you killed him/her?
¿Se dio cuenta que lo/la mató?
¿seh DEE-oh KWEHN-tah keh loh/lah mah-TOH?

Helpful Phrases

Along with gathering information at the scene and interviewing victims and witnesses, your investigation should also determine if the victim wants to prosecute, whether the suspect(s) can be identified if seen again, and whether the victim or witnesses will go to court to testify. Here are some phrases that will be helpful in obtaining this information.

Calm down.
Cálmese.
KAHL-meh-seh.

**Would you recognize them if you saw them
again?**
¿Los reconocería si los viera otra vez?
*¿lohs reh-koh-noh-seh-REE-ah see lohs vee-EH-rah
OH-trah vehs?*

Do you want to prosecute/report him?
¿Quiere denunciarlo/reportarlo?
¿kee-EH-reh deh-noon-see-AHR-loh/reh-pohr-TAHR-loh?

**Do you want to go to court to testify against
the suspect(s)?**
¿Quiere ir a la corte para testificar contra el sos-
pechoso/los sospechoso(s)?
*¿kee-EH-reh eer ah lah KOHR-teh PAH-rah tehs-tee-
fee-KAHR KOHN-trah ehl sohs-peh-CHOH-soh/lohs
sohs-peh-CHOH-soh(s)?*

Property Crimes

In This Chapter

- Broken/damaged item(s)
- Dealing with graffiti
- Interviewing victims of stolen vehicles
- Burglaries, thefts, and shoplifting

Property crimes cover a wide variety of investigations. The crimes covered in this chapter are some of the most common property crimes that law enforcement personnel are called upon to investigate.

Broken/Damaged Item

Investigating an item that has been broken or damaged usually falls under the crime of criminal damage. Questions for both the victim and the suspect are included here.

Questions for Victims

Usually, for prosecution purposes, the most important information is knowing who the property belongs to and how much it's worth.

Is this yours?
¿Es esto de usted?
¿ehs EHS-toh deh oo-STEHD?

Did you see him/her break this item?
¿Lo/la vio romper este objeto?
¿loh/lah VEE-oh rohm-PEHR EHS-teh ohb-HEH-toh?

How much is it worth?
¿Cuánto cuesta?
¿KWAHN-toh KWEHS-tah?

Was all the damage done during this incident?
¿Todo el daño fue causado durante el incidente?
¿TOH-doh ehl DAH-nyoh fweh kah-oo-SAH-doh doo-RAHN-teh ehl een-see-DEHN-teh?

When did you purchase the item?
¿Cuándo compró usted este objeto?
¿KWAHN-doh kohm-PROH oo-STEHD EHS-teh ohb-HEH-toh?

Do you have the receipt?
¿Tiene el recibo?
¿tee-EH-neh ehl reh-SEE-boh?

Questions for Suspects

During your interview, try to obtain information that will show whether the suspect will admit to the crime and/or whether he/she claims any ownership of the item.

Did you break this item?
¿Rompió usted este objeto?
¿rohm-pee-OH oo-STEHD EHS-teh ohb-HEH-toh?

Did you intend to break this item?
¿Fue su intención romperlo?
¿fweh soo een-tehn-see-OHN rohm-PEHR-loh?

Who owns it?
¿De quién es?
¿deh kee-EHN ehs?

How much do you think it is worth?
¿Cuánto piensa que cuesta?
¿KWAHN-toh pee-EHN-sah keh KWEHS-tah?

Graffiti

Graffiti is a crime. Graffiti is when someone paints or draws on someone else's property, whether that property is a fence, a building, etc. Here are some questions to ask to investigate this crime.

Questions for Victims/Witnesses

Graffiti crimes plague many communities. Determining the victim of the crime, or who owns the property, is sometimes challenging but pertinent for prosecution.

Did you see him/her painting?
¿Usted lo/la vio pintando?
¿oo-STEHD loh/lah VEE-oh peen-TAHN-doh?

Are you positive it was this person?
¿Está seguro/a que fue esta persona?
¿ehs-TAH seh-GOO-roh/rah keh fweh EHS-tah pehr-SOH-nah?

Show me what you saw him/her paint.
Muéstreme lo que usted vio que esta persona pintó.
moo-EHS-treh-meh loh keh oo-STEHD vee-OH keh EHS-tah pehr-SOH-nah peen-TOH.

Do you own this property?
¿Usted es dueño/a de esta propiedad?
¿oo-STEHD ehs DWEH-nyoh/nyah deh EHS-tah proh-pee-eh-DAHD?

Do you know who owns this property?
¿Sabe quién es el dueño de esta propiedad?
¿SAH-beh kee-EHN ehs ehl DWEH-nyoh/nyah deh EHS-tah proh-pee-eh-DAHD?

Questions for Suspects

It's important to ensure the prosecution of these crimes, especially because graffiti is so prevalent in parts of our communities. Here are some questions to try to establish the suspect's guilt.

Let me see your hands.
Déjeme ver sus manos.
DEH-heh-meh vehr soos MAH-nohs.

Did you draw this?
¿Usted dibujó esto?
¿oo-STEHD dee-boo-HOH EHS-toh?

Did you know it is illegal to do this?
¿Sabe que es ilegal hacer esto?
¿SAH-beh keh ehs ee-leh-GAHL ah-SEHR EHS-toh?

Where did you get the paint/spray paint?
¿De dónde sacó la pintura/el aerosol?
¿deh DOHN-deh sah-KOH lah peen-TOO-rah/
ehl ah-eh-roh-SOHL?

Are you in a gang?
¿Pertenece usted a una pandilla?
¿pehr-teh-NEH-seh oo-STEHD ah OO-nah pahn-
DEE-yah?

Common slang for "gang" is *ganga*
(*GAHN-gah*). Gangs often graffiti
neighborhoods to establish their territories.
Thus, graffiti and *gangas* usually go hand in
hand.

The name of your gang?
¿Cuál es el nombre de su pandilla?
¿KWAHL ehs ehl NOHM-breh deh soo pahn-DEE-yah?

Stolen Vehicles

When called to investigate a stolen vehicle, use the
following questions to interview the victim. From
these questions, you should be able to get enough

information to complete a basic report and determine if the vehicle was indeed stolen or if it was repossessed. Ideally, you'll be able to locate a suspect, too.

Questions for Victims

Establishing a time frame helps determine if you need assistance conducting an immediate search for the vehicle. Once that is determined, you need the identifying characteristics, especially the license plate or vehicle identification number.

How long has the vehicle been missing?
¿Hace cuánto tiempo que desapareció el vehículo?
¿AH-seh KWAHN-toh tee-EHM-poh keh deh-sah-pah-reh-see-OH ehl veh-HEE-koo-loh?

What is the license plate of the vehicle?
¿Cuál es el número de la placa del vehículo?
¿KWAHL ehs ehl NOO-meh-roh deh lah PLAH-kah dehl veh-HEE-koo-loh?

Is the vehicle registered in your name?
¿El vehículo está registrado a su nombre?
¿ehl veh-HEE-koo-loh ehs-TAH reh-hee-STRAH-doh ah soo NOHM-breh?

To whom is the vehicle registered?
¿A nombre de quién está registrado el vehículo?
¿ah NOHM-breh deh kee-EHN ehs-TAH reh-hee-STRAH-doh ehl veh-HEE-koo-loh?

Do you have a copy of the title or registration here?
¿Tiene usted una copia del título o registro aquí?
¿tee-EH-neh oo-STEHD OO-nah KOH-pee-ah dehl TEE-too-loh oh reh-HEE-stroh ah-KEE?

Does anyone else have a key?
¿Alguien más tiene la llave?
¿AHL-gee-ehn MAHS tee-EH-neh lah YAH-veh?

Were the doors locked?
¿Estaban cerradas las puertas?
¿ehs-TAH-bahn sehr-RAH-dahs lahs poo-EHR-tahs?

 Common street slang or Spanglish for "to lock" is *loquear (loh-KEE-ahr).*

Was the key in the ignition?
¿Estaba la llave puesta en el arranque?
¿ehs-TAH-bah lah YAH-veh PWEH-stah ehn ehl ahr-RAHN-keh?

Is the vehicle paid off?
¿El vehículo estaba completamente pagado?
¿ehl veh-HEE-koo-loh ehs-TAH-bah kohm-pleh-tah-MEHN-teh pah-GAH-doh?

Who is your loan with?
¿Con qué compañía tiene el préstamo?
¿kohn KEH kohm-pah-NEE-ah tee-EH-neh ehl PREHS-tah-moh?

Did you have personal property inside the vehicle?
¿Tenía usted propiedad personal adentro del vehículo?
¿teh-NEE-ah oo-STEHD proh-pee-eh-DAHD pehr-soh-NAHL ah-DEHN-troh dehl veh-HEE-koo-loh?

Questions for Suspects

The following two questions are usually the most important for prosecution purposes.

Did you know the vehicle was stolen?
¿Sabía usted que el vehículo era robado?
¿sah-BEE-ah oo-STEHD keh ehl veh-HEE-koo-loh EH-rah roh-BAH-doh?

Did you steal the vehicle?
¿Usted robó el vehículo?
¿oo-STEHD roh-BOH ehl veh-HEE-koo-loh?

Burglary

Burglary refers to the act of a suspect breaking into a location and committing a crime inside, usually stealing items or another felony.

Questions for Victims

Probably two of the most important facts to obtain regarding a burglary are the items taken and the time frame in which they were taken.

Are you the resident/owner of the house/ business?
¿Es usted el residente/dueño de la casa/el negocio?
¿ehs oo-STEHD ehl reh-see-DEHN-teh/doo-EH-nyoh deh lah KAH-sah/ehl neh-GOH-see-oh?

Were you home at the time of the burglary?
¿Estaba en la casa en el momento del robo?
¿eh-STAH-bah ehn lah KAH-sah ehn ehl moh-MEHN-toh dehl ROH-boh?

Did you see the suspect?
¿Vio al sospechoso?
¿vee-OH ahl sohs-peh-CHOH-soh?

At what time did you leave the house/location?
¿A qué hora salió de la casa?
¿ah KEH OH-rah sah-lee-OH deh lah KAH-sah?

At what time did you return?
¿A qué hora regresó?
¿ah KEH OH-rah reh-greh-SOH?

How did the suspect get in?
¿Cómo entró el sospechoso?
¿KOH-moh ehn-TROH ehl sohs-peh-CHOH-soh?

Were the doors and windows locked?
¿Estaban las puertas y ventanas cerradas con llave?
¿ehs-TAH-bahn lahs poo-EHR-tahs ee vehn-TAH-nahs sehr-RAH-dahs kohn YAH-veh?

**Does anyone else have a key for the house/
business?**

¿Alguien más tiene la llave de la casa/del negocio?

*¿AHL-gee-EHN MAHS tee-EH-neh lah YAH-veh deh
lah KAH-sah/dehl neh-GOH-see-oh?*

Do you think the suspect touched anything?

¿Le parece que el sospechoso tocó algo?

*¿leh pah-REH-seh keh ehl sohs-peh-CHOH-soh toh-
KOH AHL-goh?*

What?

¿Qué?

¿KEH?

What are you missing?

¿Qué le falta?

¿KEH leh FAHL-tah?

Do you have an idea who the suspect is?

¿Tiene idea de quién es el sospechoso?

*¿tee-EH-neh ee-DEH-ah deh kee-EHN ehs ehl sohs-
peh-CHOH-soh?*

Who?

¿Quién?

¿kee-EHN?

Are there witnesses?

¿Hay testigos?

¿ai tehs-TEE-gohs?

Questions for Suspects

Although property crimes usually have a low clear-
ance rate, think positive.

Do you have keys to enter the building/house?
¿Tiene usted las llaves para entrar al edificio/a la casa?
¿tee-EH-neh oo-STEHD lahs YAH-vehs PAH-rah ehn-TRAHR ahl eh-dee-FEE-see-oh/ah lah KAH-sah?

Did you illegally enter this building/house?
¿Entró usted ilegalmente a este edificio/esta casa?
¿ehn-TROH oo-STEHD ee-leh-gahl-MEHN-teh ah EHS-teh eh-dee-FEE-see-oh/EHS-tah KAH-sah?

Did you steal anything from inside?
¿Robó usted algo de adentro?
¿roh-BOH oo-STEHD AHL-goh deh ah-DEHN-troh?

Theft

Theft includes crimes wherein a suspect takes the property of another without using force or a weapon, or removing the property from an area where the public has access.

Questions for Victims

To investigate a theft, you have to prove ownership of the item stolen. Here are some questions that will help.

What was stolen?
¿Qué se robaron?
¿KEH seh roh-BAH-rohn?

How much was it worth?
¿Cuál era el valor?
¿KWAHL EH-rah ehl vah-LOHR?

Where exactly was it stolen from?

¿De dónde se lo/la robaron?

¿deh DOHN-deh seh loh/lah roh-BAH-rohn?

Was it secured?

¿Tenía algún tipo de seguro puesto?

¿teh-NEE-ah ahl-GOON TEE-poh deh seh-GOO-roh PWEHS-toh?

Do you own the property taken?

¿Usted es el dueño de la propiedad que se llevaron?

¿oo-STEHD ehs ehl DWEH-nyoh deh lah proh-pee-eh-DAHD KEH seh yeh-VAH-rohn?

Can you prove the property belongs to you?

¿Puede probar que la propiedad es suya?

¿PWEH-deh proh-BAHR keh lah proh-pee-eh-DAHD ehs SOO-yah?

Do you have surveillance cameras?

¿Tiene cámaras de seguridad?

¿tee-EH-neh KAH-mah-rahs deh seh-goo-ree-DAHD?

Questions for Suspects

Proving a theft from a business is usually pretty easy. However, proving theft from a private party is a bit more difficult.

Did you steal the object/these objects?

¿Robó usted este objeto/estos objetos?

¿roh-BOH oo-STEHD EHS-teh ohb-HEH-toh/EHS-tohs ohb-HEH-tohs?

Where did you steal it from?
¿De dónde lo/los robó?
¿deh DOHN-deh lo/lohs roh-BOH?

Shoplifting

Oftentimes, when officers respond to a shoplifting call, the suspect is already in custody thanks to store security. Therefore, the following questions are for both the victim and the suspect.

Questions for Victims

You need to obtain some basic, yet pertinent, information from the store. This allows you to establish exactly what the suspect will be charged with.

Did you see him/her take the item?
¿Usted lo/la vio tomar la mercadería?
¿oo-STEHD loh/lah vee-OH toh-MAHR lah mehr-kah-deh-REE-ah?

Did he/she walk past the register?
¿Pasó él/ella más allá de la caja registradora?
¿pah-SOH EHL/eyah MAHS ah-YAH deh lah KAH-hah reh-hee-strah-DOH-rah?

Did he/she walk past the front door?
¿Pasó él/ella más allá de la puerta del frente?
¿pah-SOH EHL/eyah MAHS ah-YAH deh lah PWEHR-tah dehl FREHN-teh?

Where did you stop him/her?
¿Dónde lo/la paró?
¿DOHN-deh loh/lah pah-ROH?

Did he/she make any attempt to pay?
¿Tuvo él/ella la intención de pagar?
¿TOO-voh EHL/eyah lah een-tehn-see-OHN deh pah-GAHR?

Where did he/she conceal the items(s)?
¿En dónde escondió la mercadería?
¿ehn DOHN-deh ehs-kohn-dee-OH lah mehr-kah-deh-REE-ah?

How much is the stolen property worth?
¿Cuánto vale la mercadería que se robaron?
¿KWAHN-toh VAH-leh lah mehr-kah-deh-REE-ah keh seh roh-BAH-rohn?

Do you have surveillance video?
¿Tiene video-cámaras de seguridad?
¿tee-EH-neh vee-deh-oh-KAH-mah-rahs deh seh-goo-ree-DAHD?

Can I see the video?
¿Puedo ver el video?
¿PWEH-doh vehr ehl vee-DEH-oh?

Can I take the video for evidence?
¿Puedo llevarme el video como evidencia?
¿PWEH-doh yeh-VAHR-meh ehl vee-DEH-oh KOH-moh eh-vee-DEHN-see-ah?

Will the store prosecute?
¿La tienda va a poner cargos en los tribunales/
la corte?
*¿lah tee-EHN-dah vah ah poh-NEHR KAHR-gohs ehn
lohs tree-boo-NAH-lehs/lah KOHR-teh?*

Questions for Suspects

When talking to the suspect, certain information
will help determine exactly what to charge him/her
with.

What did you steal?
¿Qué se robó?
¿KEH seh roh-BOH?

Have you ever stolen items from a store before?
¿Se ha robado mercadería de una tienda alguna vez?
*¿seh ah roh-BAH-doh mehr-kah-deh-REE-ah deh OO-
nah tee-EHN-dah ahl-GOO-nah vehs?*

**Did you enter the store with the intention of
stealing?**
¿Entró usted a la tiende con el propósito de robar?
*¿ehn-TROH oo-STEHD ah lah tee-EHN-dah kohn ehl
proh-POH-see-toh deh roh-BAHR?*

**Did you bring that bag with you to use for
stealing items?**
¿Trajo usted esa bolsa para usarla para robar mercadería?
*¿TRAH-hoh oo-STEHD EH-sah BOHL-sah PAH-rah
oo-SAHR-lah PAH-rah roh-BAHR mehr-kah-deh-
REE-ah?*

Did you make any attempt to pay?
¿Trató usted de pagar por esto?
¿trah-TOH oo-STEHD deh pah-GAHR pohr EHS-toh?

Do you have any money on you right now?
¿Tiene dinero aquí con usted?
¿tee-EH-neh dee-NEH-roh ah-KEE kohn oo-STEHD?

Helpful Phrases

When investigating a property crime, it's obviously
important to know who owns the item in question,
whether it's a television, a car, or a building. These
questions can be applied to most property crimes.

Does this object/these objects belong to you?
¿Este objeto/estos objetos le pertenece/n a usted?
*¿EHS-teh ohb-HEH-toh/EHS-tohs ohb-HEH-tohs leh
pehr-teh-NEH-seh/sehn ah oo-STEHD?*

An easier way to ask this question:

Is this object yours?
¿Es este objeto suyo?
¿ehs EHS-teh ohb-HEH-toh SOO-yoh?

Is anything damaged?
¿Algo está dañado?
¿AHL-goh ehs-TAH dah-NYAH-doh?

Leave the building.
Salga del edificio.
SAHL-gah dehl eh-dee-FEE-see-oh.

Drugs, Missing Persons, and Other Crimes

In This Chapter

- Dealing with drug cases
- Missing persons
- Trespassing
- Prostitution and other crimes

Law enforcement professionals investigate so many types of crimes. We've looked at several in the preceding chapters. In this chapter, we look at a few more fairly common incidents first responders might have to investigate, including drug possession and sale, missing persons, trespassing, prostitution, and animal cruelty cases.

Drug Possession and Sale

Different challenges exist when interviewing someone whose drugs were found on his/her person, in his/her vehicle, or in his/her residence. The questions to prove possession for sale are also unique. The following questions should aid you in your investigation.

Possession Cases on Foot

The following questions refer to making contact with a person and subsequently finding drugs on them.

Can I talk to you?
¿Puedo hablar con usted?
¿PWEH-doh ah-BLAHR kohn oo-STEHD?

Do you have any drugs on you?
¿Usted tiene alguna droga en su persona?
¿oo-STEHD tee-EH-neh ahl-GOO-nah DROH-grahs ehn soo pehr-SOH-nah?

Can I search you?
¿Le puedo esculcar/revisar?
¿leh PWEH-doh ehs-kool-KAHR/reh-vee-SAHR?

Can I search you for drugs or weapons?
¿Le puedo esculcar/revisar por drogas o armas?
¿leh PWEH-doh ehs-kool-KAHR/reh-vee-SAHR pohr DROH-gahs oh AHR-mahs?

If the subject seems not to understand the word *revisar* (*reh-vee-SAHR*), try another word for "to search": *esculcar* (*ehs-kool-KAHR*).

What type of drugs are these?
¿Qué tipo de drogas son éstas?
¿KEH TEE-poh deh DROH-gahs sohn EHS-tahs?

Are the drugs yours?
¿Las drogas son suyas?
¿lahs DROH-gahs sohn SOO-yahs?

Where did you get them?
¿Dónde las consiguió?
¿DOHN-deh lahs kohn-see-gee-OH?

How much did you pay for the drugs?
¿Cuánto pagó por las drogas?
¿KWAHN-toh pah-GOH pohr lahs DROH-gahs?

Is this your shirt?
¿Ésta es su camisa? *Or:* ¿Es su camisa?
¿EHS-tah ehs soo kah-MEE-sah? Or: ¿Ehs soo kah-MEE-sah?

Are these your pants?
¿Son sus pantalones?
¿sohn soos pahn-tah-LOH-nehs?

Types of Drugs

English	Spanish	Pronunciation
alcohol	alcohol	*abl-KOH-bobl*
amphetamine	amfetamina	*abm-feb-tab-MEE-nab*
cocaine	blanco	*BLAHN-kob*
	coca	*KOH-kab*
	cocaína	*kob-kab-EE-nab*
	la huera	*lab oo-EH-rab*
	nieve	*nee-EH-veb*
	perico	*peb-REE-kob*
	polvo	*POHL-vob*
crack cocaine	piedra	*pee-EH-drab*
hallucinogen	alucinógeno	*ab-loo-see-NOH-beb-nob*
heroin	cargada	*kabr-GAH-dab*
	chiva	*CHEE-vab*
	heroína	*ebr-ob-EE-nab*

English	Spanish	Pronunciation
	llanta	*YAHN-tah*
	negro	*NEH-groh*
inhalants	inhalantes	*een-hah-LAHN-tehs*
marijuana	mota	*MOH-tah*
	marijuana	*mah-ree-hoo-AH-nah*
methamphetamine	cristal	*krees-TAHL*
	G	*gee*
	hielo	*ee-EH-loh*
	meta	*MEH-tah*
	ventana	*vehn-TAH-nah*
	vidrio	*VEE-dree-oh*
mushrooms	hongos	*OHN-gohs*
prescription drugs	recetas médicas	*reh-SEH-tahs MEH-dee-kahs*

Are these your socks?
¿Son sus calcetines?
¿sohn soos kahl-seh-TEE-nehs?

Are these your shoes?
¿Son sus zapatos?
¿sohn soos sah-PAH-tohs?

Is this your cowboy hat?
¿Es su sombrero?
¿ehs soo sohm-BREH-roh?

Is this your baseball hat?
¿Es su cachucha/gorra?
¿ehs soo kah-CHOO-chah/GOHR-rah?

Possession Cases in Vehicles

These questions refer to making contact with a subject in a vehicle and subsequently finding drugs in the vehicle.

Is this your vehicle?
¿Es su vehículo?
¿ehs soo veh-HEE-koo-loh?

Does anyone else drive the vehicle?
¿Alguien más maneja el vehículo?
¿AHL-gee-ehn MAHS mah-NEH-hah ehl veh-HEE-koo-loh?

Who?
¿Quién?
¿kee-EHN?

Who does the vehicle belong to? *Or:* **Who is the owner?**

¿A quién le pertenece el vehículo? *Or:* ¿Quién es el dueño?

¿ah kee-EHN leh pehr-teh-NEH-seh ehl veh-HEE-koo-loh? Or: ¿kee-EHN ehs ehl DWEH-nyoh?

What is his/her name?

¿Cómo se llama él/ella?

¿KOH-moh seh YAH-mah EHL/eyah?

How long have you been driving the vehicle?

¿Cuánto tiempo ha manejado el vehículo?

¿KWAHN-toh tee-EHM-poh ah mah-neh-HAH-doh ehl veh-HEE-koo-loh?

Days?

¿Días?

¿DEE-ahs?

Weeks?

¿Semanas?

¿seh-MAH-nahs?

Months?

¿Meses?

¿MEH-sehs?

What time did you start driving the vehicle today/tonight?

¿A qué hora empezó a manejar el vehículo hoy/esta noche?

¿ah KEH OH-rah ehm-peh-SOH ah mah-neh-HAHR ehl veh-HEE-koo-loh oi/EHS-tah NOH-cheh?

Can I search the vehicle?
¿Puedo revisar el vehículo?
¿PWEH-doh reh-vee-SAHR ehl veh-HEE-koo-loh?

Can I search the vehicle for drugs or weapons?
¿Puedo revisar el vehículo por drogas o armas?
¿PWEH-doh reh-vee-SAHR ehl veh-HEE-koo-loh pohr DROH-gahs oh AHR-mahs?

Did you know the drugs were in the vehicle?
¿Sabía usted que las drogas estaban adentro del vehículo?
¿sah-BEE-ah oo-STEHD keh lahs DROH-gahs ehs-TAH-bahn ah-DEHN-troh dehl veh-HEE-koo-loh?

Will your fingerprints be on the bags?
¿Estaran sus huellas digitales marcadas en las bolsas?
¿ehs-tah-RAHN soos oo-EH-yahs dee-hee-TAHL-ehs ehn lahs BOHL-sahs?

Possession Cases in Residences

The following questions apply to incidents where drugs are located inside a residence, whether they be in plain view or you find them via a search warrant.

Is this your house?
¿Ésta es su casa?
¿EHS-tah ehs soo KAH-sah?

How long have you lived here in this house/ apartment?
¿Cuánto tiempo ha vivido en esta casa/apartamento?
¿KWAHN-toh tee-EHM-poh ah vee-VEE-doh ehn EHS-tah KAH-sah/ah-pahr-tah-MEHN-toh?

Who else lives here?

¿Quién más vive aquí?

¿kee-EHN mahs VEE-veh ah-KEE?

Do you pay rent?

¿Paga renta/alquiler?

¿PAH-gah REHN-tah/ahl-kee-LEHR?

Does anyone else have keys to the house/ apartment?

¿Quién más tiene las llaves de su casa/apartamento?

¿kee-EHN mahs tee-EH-neh lahs YAH-vehs deh soo KAH-sah/ah-pahr-tah-MEHN-toh?

Their name?

¿Su nombre?

¿soo NOHM-breh?

Are there drugs in the house?

¿Hay drogas adentro de la casa?

¿ai DROH-gahs ah-DEHN-troh deh lah KAH-sah?

Are there any weapons in the house?

¿Hay armas adentro de la casa?

¿ai AHR-mahs ah-DEHN-troh deh lah KAH-sah?

Can we search the house for drugs or weapons?

¿Podemos revisar su casa por drogas o armas?

¿poh-DEH-mohs reh-vee-SAHR soo KAH-sah pohr DROH-gahs oh AHR-mahs?

Can we look to see if there are any drugs or weapons in your house?

¿Podemos buscar si hay drogas o armas en su casa?

¿poh-DEH-mohs boos-KAHR see ai DROH-gahs oh AHR-mahs ehn soo KAH-sah?

Possession for Sale

The following questions apply to situations where the amount of drugs found exceed the amount for personal use. Hopefully, the questions will help establish your possession for sale case.

Do you sell drugs?
¿Vende drogas?
¿VEHN-deh DROH-gahs?

What type?
¿Qué tipo(s)?
¿KEH TEE-poh(s)?

Where do you get your drugs?
¿Dónde consigue las drogas?
¿DOHN-deh kohn-SEE-geh lahs DROH-gahs?

What type of drugs does he/she sell?
¿Qué tipo de drogas vende él/ella?
¿KEH TEE-poh deh DROH-gahs VEHN-deh EHL/ eyah?

From whom do you buy your drugs?
¿Cómo se llama la persona que le vendió las drogas?
¿KOH-moh seh YAH-mah lah pehr-SOH-nah keh leh vehn-dee-OH lahs DROH-gahs?

How do you contact him/her?
¿Cómo se pone en contacto con él/ella?
¿KOH-moh seh POH-neh ehn kohn-TAHK-toh kohn EHL/eyah?

Telephone number?
¿Número de teléfono?
¿NOO-meh-roh deh teh-LEH-foh-noh?

What type of vehicle does he/she drive?
¿Qué tipo de carro maneja él/ella?
*¿KEH TEE-poh deh KAHR-roh mah-NEH-hah EHL/
eyah?*

Color?
¿Color?
¿koh-LOHR?

Where does he/she live?
¿Dónde vive él/ella?
¿DOHN-deh VEE-veh EHL/eyah?

How much do you make every day?
¿Cuánto gana al día?
¿KWAHN-toh GAH-nah ahl DEE-ah?

How much do you make a week?
¿Cuánto gana a la semana?
¿KWAHN-toh GAH-nah ah lah seh-MAH-nah?

Do you have any other source of income?
¿Tiene otras formas de ingresos?
*¿tee-EH-neh OH-trahs FOHR-mahs deh een-GREH-
sohs?*

Missing Persons

Missing persons investigations can range from a
runaway person, an elderly person with Alzheimer's,
or a possible kidnapping. The following questions
should assist with any of these investigations.

When was the last time you saw _____?
The approximate time.
¿Cuándo fue la última vez que usted vio a _____?
La hora aproximada.
¿KWAHN-doh fweh lah OOL-tee-mah vehs keh oo-STEHD vee-OH ah _____? lah OH-rah ah-prohx-ee-MAH-dah.

Where did you see him/her?
¿Dónde lo/la vio?
¿DOHN-deh loh/lah vee-OH?

When was he/she supposed to return home?
¿Cuándo se suponía que regresara a la casa?
¿KWAHN-doh seh soo-poh-NEE-ah keh reh-greh-SAH-rah ah lah KAH-sah?

Has he/she ever run away or gone missing before?
¿Alguna vez se ha escapado o perdido?
¿ahl-GOO-nah vehs seh ah ehs-kah-PAH-doh oh pehr-DEE-doh?

Is it possible he/she ran away?
¿Es posible que se haya escapado?
¿ehs poh-SEE-bleh keh seh AH-yah ehs-kah-PAH-doh?

Where was he/she located at that time?
¿Dónde estaba él/ella en ese momento?
¿DOHN-deh ehs-TAH-bah EHL/eyah ehn EH-seh moh-MEHN-toh?

Remember to ask to check their house for the missing person before searching elsewhere:

Can I make sure he/she is not inside your house?
¿Puedo asegurarme de que no esté adentro de la casa?
¿PWEH-doh ah-seh-goo-RAHR-meh deh keh noh ehs-TEH ah-DEHN-troh deh lah KAH-sah?

What was he/she wearing when last seen?
¿Qué llevaba puesto la última vez que lo/la vio?
¿KEH yeh-VAH-bah PWEHS-toh lah OOL-tee-mah vehs keh loh/lah vee-OH?

Is he/she on medication?
¿Está él/ella tomando medicamentos?
¿ehs-TAH EHL/eyah toh-MAHN-doh meh-dee-kah-MEHN-tohs?

Where would he/she go?
¿A dónde piensa que pudiera ir?
¿ah DOHN-deh pee-EHN-sah keh poo-dee-EH-rah eer?

Have you checked any friends' or relatives' houses?
¿Ha revisado la casa de parientes o amigos?
¿ah reh-vee-SAH-doh lah KAH-sah deh pah-ree-EHN-tehs oh ah-MEE-gohs?

What are those addresses?
¿Cuáles son las direcciones?
¿KWAHL-ehs sohn lahs dee-rehk-see-OHN-ehs?

Does he/she have a girlfriend/boyfriend?
¿Tiene él/ella un novio/una novia?
*¿tee-EH-neh EHL/eyah oon NOH-vee-oh/OO-nah
NOH-vee-ah?*

Has he/she received any threats lately?
¿A él/ella le han amenazado ultimamente?
*¿ah EHL/eyah leh ahn ah-mehn-ah-SAH-doh ool-tee-
mah-MEHN-teh?*

**Do you know anyone who would like to harm
him/her?**
¿Sabe si alguien quiere hacerle daño?
*¿SAH-beh see AHL-gee-ehn kee-EH-reh ah-SEHR-leh
DAH-nyoh?*

Do you have a recent photograph?
¿Tiene alguna fotografía reciente?
*¿tee-EH-neh ahl-GOO-nah foh-toh-grah-FEE-ah reh-
see-EHN-teh?*

Trespassing

When dealing with someone trespassing on private
property, it's important to be sure he or she under-
stands they cannot return to the property or they
will be arrested.

Have you ever been trespassed from this property before?

¿Alguna vez ha entrado sin permiso en esta propiedad?

¿ahl-GOO-nah vehs ah ehn-TRAH-doh seen pehr-MEE-soh ehn EHS-tah proh-pee-eh-DAHD?

How long ago?

¿Hace cuánto tiempo?

¿AH-seh KWAHN-toh tee-EHM-poh?

Did someone ask you to leave the property today?

¿Alguien le ha dicho que saliera de esta propiedad hoy?

¿AHL-gee-ehn leh ah DEE-choh keh sah-lee-EH-rah deh EHS-tah proh-pee-eh-DAHD?

Who?

¿Quién?

¿kee-EHN?

Did you know that if you returned to this property, you would be arrested for trespassing?

¿Sabía usted que si volvía a esta propiedad, usted sería arrestado/a por entrar sin permiso?

¿sah-BEE-ah oo-STEHD keh see vohl-VEE-ah ah EHS-tah proh-pee-eh-DAHD, oo-STEHD seh-REE-ah ahr-rehs-TAH-doh/dah pohr ehn-TRAHR seen pehr-MEE-soh?

Do you understand that if you return to this property, you will be arrested for trespassing?
¿Entiende usted que si vuelve a esta propiedad, usted será arrestado/a por entrar sin permiso?
¿ehn-tee-EHN-deh oo-STEHD keh see voo-EHL-veh ah EHS-tah proh-pee-eh-DAHD, oo-STEHD seh-RAH ahr-rehs-TAH-doh/dah pohr ehn-TRAHR seen pehr-MEE-soh?

Prostitution

When talking to prostitutes, it's often important to establish that he or she is actively working the street as a prostitute. Whether this interview is to document his or her activity for future arrests or for a current arrest, certain information is pertinent to establish.

Are you working the street (as a prostitute)?
¿Trabaja en la calle (como prostituta)?
¿trah-BAH-hah ehn lah KAH-yeh (KOH-moh prohs-tee-TOO-tah)?

How long have you been a prostitute?
¿Hace cuánto que es usted prostituta?
¿AH-seh KWAHN-toh keh ehs oo-STEHD prohs-tee-TOO-tah?

How much do you make a night?
¿Cuánto gana por noche?
¿KWAHN-toh GAH-nah pohr NOH-cheh?

How much do you charge for sex?
¿Cuánto cobra por tener relaciones sexuales?
¿KWAHN-toh KOH-brah pohr TEH-nehr reh-lah-see-OHN-ehs sehx-oo-AHL-ehs?

How much do you charge for oral sex?
¿Cuánto cobra por sexo oral?
¿KWAHN-toh KOH-brah pohr SEHX-oh oh-RAHL?

Do you work any other areas?
¿Trabaja usted en otra áreas?
¿trah-BAH-hah oo-STEHD ehn OH-trah AH-ree-ahs?

Do you have a pimp?
¿Tiene usted un hombre que le hace trabajar de esto?
¿tee-EH-neh oo-STEHD oon OHM-breh keh leh AH-seh trah-bah-HAHR deh EHS-toh?

Street Slang

There is no exact word for *pimp* in Spanish. Some slang terminology from Mexico and Argentina are *padrote* (*pah-DROH-teh*) and *cafigio* (*kah-FEE-gee-oh*).

What is his name?
¿Cómo se llama él?
¿KOH-moh seh YAH-mah EHL?

What does he drive?
¿Qué carro/auto maneja?
¿KEH KAHR-roh/AH-oo-toh mah-NEH-hah?

Cruelty to Animals

Depending on state statutes, cruelty to animals can range from malnourished animals, cock or dog fighting, dead animals due to mistreatment, and a variety of other scenarios. In any of these scenarios, you must establish certain criteria about the animal.

Is this your animal?
¿Este animal es suyo?
¿EHS-teh ah-nee-MAHL ehs SOO-yoh?

Types of Animals

English	Spanish	Pronunciation
cat	gato	*GAH-toh*
dog	perro	*PEHR-roh*
horse	caballo	*kah-BAH-yoh*
rooster	gallo	*GAH-yoh*

How old is the animal?
¿Cuántos años tiene el animal?
¿KWAHN-tohs AH-nyohs tee-EH-neh ehl ah-nee-MAHL?

How long have you owned the animal?
¿Por cuánto tiempo ha tenido este animal?
¿pohr KWAHN-toh tee-EHM-poh ah teh-NEE-doh EHS-teh ah-nee-MAHL?

When did you feed your animal last?
¿Cuándo fue la última vez que le dio de comer?
¿KWAHN-doh fweh lah OOL-tee-mah vehs keh leh dee-OH deh koh-MEHR?

When was the last time you gave your animal water?
¿Cuándo fue la última vez que le dio agua?
¿KWAHN-doh fweh lah OOL-tee-mah vehs keh leh dee-OH AH-gwah?

How long has your animal been tied up here?
¿Hace cuánto que su animal ha estado atado aquí?
¿AH-seh KWAHN-toh keh soo ah-nee-MAHL ah ehs-TAH-doh ah-TAH-doh ah-KEE?

How long has your animal been dead?
¿Hace cuánto que su animal murió?
¿AH-seh KWAHN-toh keh soo ah-nee-MAHL moo-ree-OH?

Do you force your animal to fight?
¿Usted ha obligado a su animal a pelear?
¿oo-STEHD ah oh-blee-GAH-doh ah soo ah-nee-MAHL ah peh-leh-AHR?

Do you own any other animals?
¿Tiene otros animales?
¿tee-EH-neh OH-trohs ah-nee-MAHL-ehs?

Helpful Phrases

Here are some final questions to assist you with investigations for the crimes covered in this chapter.

Do you have anything sharp in your pockets?
¿Usted tiene alguna cosa afilada en sus bolsillos?
¿oo-STEHD tee-EH-neh ahl-GOO-nah KOH-sah ah-fee-LAH-dah ehn soos bohl-SEE-yohs?

Have you seen this person today or recently?
¿Ha visto a esta persona hoy o recientemente?
¿ah VEES-toh ah EHS-tah pehr-SOH-nah oi oh reh-see-ehn-teh-MEHN-teh?

Did you know you were committing a crime?
¿Sabía usted que estaba cometiendo un delito?
¿sah-BEE-ah oo-STEHD keh ehs-TAH-bah koh-meh-tee-EHN-doh oon deh-LEE-toh?

Have you been arrested for this crime before?
¿Ha sido arrestado/a por este delito anteriormente?
¿ah SEE-doh ahr-rehs-TAH-doh/dah pohr EHS-teh deh-LEE-toh ahn-teh-ree-ohr-MEHN-teh?

Immigration Crimes

In This Chapter

- Determining legal status
- Transportation and housing of illegals
- Extortion of illegals

Immigration crimes cover a variety of scenarios, including the transportation of illegal aliens, houses where illegal aliens are transported to and from, creation of false identities for entry, and kidnapping for extortion once the illegal aliens have arrived in the country. This chapter gives you the words and phrases you need to deal with these situations.

Illegal Entry

The following questions are designed to be used by officers who work border crossings or immigration enforcement at airports, etc., to obtain the appropriate documentation for legal entry. These also work for officers attempting to determine resident status.

What country are you from?
¿De qué país es usted?
¿deh KEH pah-EES ehs oo-STEHD?

What state are you from in Mexico?
¿De qué estado de México es usted?
¿deh KEH ehs-TAH-doh deh MEH-hee-koh ehs oo-STEHD?

What city/town/ranch?
¿De qué ciudad/pueblo/rancho?
¿deh KEH see-oo-DAHD/PWEH-bloh/RAHN-choh?

Stop Sign

Individuals from Mexico often refer to their location of origin in the country as a "ranch" if they're not from the city. Be sure to obtain the "ranch" name.

Do you have a visa?
¿Tiene usted visa?
¿tee-EH-neh oo-STEHD VEE-sah?

Do you have a passport?
¿Tiene usted un pasaporte?
¿tee-EH-neh oo-STEHD oon pah-sah-POHR-teh?

What is your intended destination?
¿Cuál es su destino final?
¿KWAHL ehs soo dehs-TEE-noh fee-NAHL?

Paperwork

Illegal aliens often obtain false identifications in the United States and claim that the identifications are from their country of origin or their consulate. They often also obtain a United States identification and Social Security card illegally. You need to identify these identifications and obtain minimal information to apprehend those making the identifications.

Is this a real identification?
¿Es ésta una identificación verdadera?
¿ehs EHS-tah OO-nah ee-dehn-tee-fee-kah-see-OHN vehr-dah-DEH-rah?

This is a fake identification.
Ésta es una identificación falsa.
EHS-tah ehs OO-nah ee-dehn-tee-fee-kah-see-OHN FAHL-sah.

A common word among Mexicans for fake identification is *chueco* (*choo-EH-koh*).

Where did you purchase the identification?
¿Dónde compró esta identificación?
¿DOHN-deh kohm-PROH EHS-tah ee-dehn-tee-fee-kah-see-OHN?

How much did the identification cost?
¿Cuánto costó esta identificación?
¿KWAHN-toh kohs-TOH EHS-tah ee-dehn-tee-fee-kah-see-OHN?

Did you know it is a crime to have a fake identification?
¿Sabía usted que es un delito tener una identificación falsa?
¿sah-BEE-ah oo-STEHD keh ehs oon deh-LEE-toh teh-NEHR OO-nah ee-dehn-tee-fee-kah-see-OHN FAHL-sah?

Is this your Social Security card?
¿Ésta es su tarjeta de seguro social?
¿EHS-tah ehs soo tahr-HEH-tah deh seh-GOO-roh soh-see-AHL?

Where did you purchase the card?
¿Dónde compró la tarjeta?
¿DOHN-deh kohm-PROH lah tahr-HEH-tah?

Have you used the Social Security number at any jobs?
¿Usó usted el número del seguro social en algún trabajo?
¿oo-SOH oo-STEHD ehl NOO-meh-roh dehl seh-GOO-roh soh-see-AHL ehn ahl-GOON trah-BAH-hoh?

Illegal Smuggling Homes and Vehicles

Questions for illegal aliens found in a house, an apartment, or a vehicle are going to be the same.

Ideally, an illegal alien will assist with identifying the "coyote," or smuggler, in the group.

How long have you been in this house/ apartment?
¿Hace cuánto que está en esta casa/apartamento?
¿AH-seh KWAHN-toh keh ehs-TAH ehn EHS-tah KAH-sah/ah-pahr-tah-MEHN-toh?

From where did you start your journey?
¿De dónde viene?
¿deh DOHN-deh vee-EH-neh?

What is your final destination?
¿Cuál es su destino final?
¿KWAHL ehs soo dehs-TEE-noh fee-NAHL?

How much did you pay to cross the border?
¿Cuánto pagó para pasar la frontera?
¿KWAHN-toh pah-GOH PAH-rah pah-SAHR lah frohn-TEH-rah?

Is the coyote here now?
¿El coyote está aquí ahora?
¿ehl koh-YOH-teh ehs-TAH ah-KEE ah-OH-rah?

Keep it Simple

Along with these questions, use your observation abilities as well. Usually the coyotes in the group are better dressed than the rest and wearing footwear.

Were you provided with any documentation?
¿Le dieron alguna documentación?
¿leh dee-EH-rohn ahl-GOO-nah doh-koo-mehn-tah-see-OHN?

Extortion

Illegal aliens are often kidnapped by their original coyote or by a new coyote and charged an additional fee for their release. These calls are often referred to as kidnapping or extortion calls.

How long have you been held in this house/ apartment?
¿Hace cuánto que está en esta casa/apartamento?
¿AH-seh KWAHN-toh keh ehs-TAH ehn EHS-tah KAH-sah/ah-pahr-tah-MEHN-toh?

Are you being held here against your will?
¿Permanece aquí por la fuerza?
¿pehr-MAH-neh-seh ah-KEE pohr lah foo-EHR-sah?

How much did you originally pay to the coyote?
¿Cuánto le pagó originalmente al coyote?
¿KWAHN-toh leh pah-GOH oh-ree-hee-nahl-MEHN-teh ahl koh-YOH-teh?

Are you being charged additional money by the coyote before they will release you?
¿El coyote le está cobrando más dinero antes de dejarlo/a ir?
¿ehl koh-YOH-teh leh ehs-TAH koh-BRAHN-doh MAHS dee-NEH-roh AHN-tehs deh deh-HAHR-loh/ lah eer?

How much?
¿Cuánto?
¿KWAHN-toh?

Did you begin your trip with a different coyote?
¿Empezó usted el viaje con otro coyote?
¿ehm-peh-SOH oo-STEHD ehl vee-AH-heh kohn OH-troh koh-YOH-teh?

When did the new coyote take over?
¿Cuándo el coyote nuevo se encargó de usted?
¿KWAHN-doh ehl koh-YOH-teh noo-EH-voh seh ehn-kahr-GOH deh oo-STEHD?

How many days ago?
¿Hace cuántos días?
¿AH-seh KWAHN-tohs DEE-ahs?

What town?
¿Qué pueblo?
¿KEH poo-EH-bloh?

Did they kill anyone that you know of in the takeover? (other coyotes or illegals)
¿Usted sabe si mataron a alguien en el cambio?
(otro coyote u otro inmigrante ilegal)
¿oo-STEHD SAH-beh see mah-TAH-rohn ah AHL-gee-ehn ehn ehl KAHM-bee-oh? (OH-troh koh-YOH-teh oo OH-troh een-mee-GRAHN-teh ee-leh-GAHL)

Who are the coyotes in this group?
¿Quiénes son coyotes en este grupo?
¿kee-EHN-ehs sohn koh-YOH-tehs ehn EHS-teh GROO-poh?

Coyotes call the illegals they're transporting *pollos* (*POH-yohs*; chickens) and often consider them an expendable commodity. The coyotes who kidnap from other coyotes are sometimes referred to as a *bajador* (*bah-hah-DOHR*) or *tumbador* (*toombah-DOHR*).

Do they have weapons?
¿Tienen armas?
¿tee-EH-nehn AHR-mahs?

Did they provide you with food and water?
¿Le dieron agua y comida?
¿leh dee-EH-rohn AH-gwah ee koh-MEE-dah?

Helpful Phrases

Here are some phrases that might be unique to immigration enforcement or encountering illegal aliens during normal law enforcement duties.

I am with the police department, not immigration.
Soy del departamento de policía, no de migración.
soi dehl deh-pahr-tah-MEHN-toh deh poh-lee-SEE-ah, noh deh mee-grah-see-OHN.

I am here to help you.
Estoy aquí para ayudarle.
ehs-TOI ah-KEE PAH-rah ah-yoo-DAHR-leh.

Are you a citizen of the United States?
¿Es usted ciudadano de los Estados Unidos?
¿ehs oo-STEHD see-oo-dah-DAH-noh deh lohs ehs-TAH-dohs oo-NEE-dohs?

In what country are you a citizen?
¿De qué país es usted ciudadano?
¿deh KEH pah-EES ehs oo-STEHD see-oo-dah-DAH-noh?

Specialized Incidents

In This Chapter

- Announcing police presence
- Barricades and hostage negotiations
- Handling search warrants
- Bomb scares
- Crowd control and disaster response

Law enforcement officers are called upon to respond to a variety of incidents, some of which are more specialized than others. In this chapter, I address several different specialized incidents, from K-9 (canine) work to bomb calls to dealing with large-scale disasters.

K-9 Announcements

K-9 announcements are fairly short and sweet. The announcement is to advise anyone inside that a K-9 is getting ready to enter the building and will bite anyone inside.

_____ **Police Department!**

¡Departamento de Policía de _____!

¡deh-pahr-tah-MEHN-toh deh poh-lee-SEE-ah deh _____!

If anyone is inside this building, come out with your hands up.

Si hay alguien en este edificio, salga con las manos en alto.

see ai AHL-gee-ehn ehn EHS-teh eh-dee-FEE-see-oh, SAHL-gah kohn lahs MAH-nohs ehn AHL-toh.

If you do not, I have a dog and he will bite.

Si no lo hace, tengo un perro que lo/la morderá.

see noh loh AH-seh, TEHN-goh oon PEHR-roh keh loh/lah mohr-deh-RAH.

Barricades

Barricades can be very dangerous situations. First responders need to obtain basic information before proceeding with a plan of action. Ideally, the incident will end with no one getting hurt.

Do you have anyone with you?

¿Hay alguien con usted?

¿ai AHL-gee-ehn kohn oo-STEHD?

Do you want to harm yourself?

¿Quiere lastimarse?

¿kee-EH-reh lahs-tee-MAHR-seh?

Do you have any weapons?
¿Tiene algún arma?
¿tee-EH-neh ahl-GOON AHR-mah?

Put the weapon away.
Guarde el arma.
goo-AHR-deh ehl AHR-mah.

Come out with your hands up.
Salga con las manos arriba.
SAHL-gah kohn lahs MAH-nohs ah-REE-bah.

We want to end this peacefully.
Queremos que esto se termine en paz.
keh-REH-mohs keh EHS-toh seh tehr-MEE-neh ehn pahs.

Hostage Negotiations

The priority in hostage negotiations is the safety of the victims and their release. First responders need to try to make contact with the suspect to keep the situation calm until a fluent Spanish speaker and/or hostage negotiator arrives.

What is your name?
¿Cuál es su nombre?
¿KWAHL ehs soo NOHM-breh?

My name is _____.
Mi nombre es _____.
mee NOHM-breh ehs _____.

Tell the suspect(s) you don't speak much Spanish—"*Hablo poco español*" (*AH-bloh POH-koh ehs-pah-nyohl*)—so that when he/she is talking to you, they understand your limitations with negotiations.

How many people are with you?
¿Cuántas personas hay con usted?
¿KWAHN-tahs pehr-SOH-nahs ai kohn oo-STEHD?

Will you allow anyone to leave?
¿Va a dejar salir a alguien?
¿vah ah deh-HAHR sah-LEER ah AHL-gee-ehn?

Are any of them injured?
¿Hay alguien herido?
¿ai AHL-gee-ehn eh-REE-doh?

Will you allow the injured to leave?
¿Va a dejar salir a las personas heridas?
¿vah ah deh-HAHR sah-LEER ah lahs pehr-SOH-nahs eh-REE-dahs?

The elderly?
¿Los más ancianos/viejos?
¿lohs MAHS ahn-see-AH-nohs/vee-EH-hohs?

Children?
¿Niños?
¿NEE-nyohs?

Have you injured anyone?
¿Lastimó usted a alguien?
¿lahs-tee-MOH oo-STEHD ah AHL-gee-ehn?

Do you have any weapons?
¿Tiene armas?
¿tee-EH-neh AHR-mahs?

What kind?
¿De qué tipo?
¿deh KEH TEE-poh?

Please do not hurt anyone.
Por favor, no lastime a nadie.
pohr fah-VOHR, noh lahs-TEE-meh ah NAH-dee-eh.

Search Warrants

The primary concern on knock-and-announce
search warrants is making the proper announcement and, ideally, in the language the person being
served the warrant will understand.

_____ Police Department!
¡Departamento de Policía de _____!
¡deh-pahr-tah-MEHN-toh deh poh-lee-SEE-ah deh
_____!

We have a search warrant!
¡Tenemos una orden de cateo!
¡teh-NEH-mohs OO-nah OHR-dehn deh kah-TEH-oh!

We have an arrest warrant for _____!
¡Tenemos una orden de arresto para _____!
¡teh-NEH-mohs OO-nah OHR-dehn deh ahr-REHS-
toh PAH-rah _____!

Keep it Simple

If you encounter suspects who you need to mirandize and question, you might want to skip to Chapter 12. The complete translation of the Miranda warnings are in that chapter.

Open the door!
¡Abra la puerta!
¡AH-brah lah PWEHR-tah!

Everyone, hands on your head!
¡Todos, manos arriba!
¡TOH-dohs, MAH-nohs ahr-REE-bah!

Do not move!
¡No se muevan!
¡noh seh moo-EH-vahn!

Bomb Calls

The initial priority of a bomb call is to decide if evacuation is needed; if so, this needs to be communicated to the potential victims. If a suspect is apprehended, some key questions can help ensure the safety of others.

Potential Victims

There is a bomb in the area.
Hay una bomba en el área.
ai OO-nah BOHM-bah ehn ehl AH-ree-ah.

I need you to evacuate the area immediately.
Necesito que evacúe el área inmediatamente.
*neh-seh-SEE-toh keh eh-vah-KOO-eh ehl AH-reh-ah
een-meh-dee-ah-tah-MEHN-teh.*

Is there anyone else inside?
¿Hay alguien más adentro?
¿ai AHL-gee-ehn MAHS ah-DEHN-troh?

Are you the last person?
¿Es usted la última persona?
¿ehs oo-STEHD lah OOL-tee-mah pehr-SOH-nah?

Questions for Suspects

Is this a real bomb?
¿Ésta es una bomba de verdad?
¿EHS-tah ehs OO-nah BOHM-bah deh vehr-DAHD?

Did you make the bomb?
¿Usted hizo la bomba?
¿oo-STEHD EE-soh lah BOHM-bah?

Do you know when it will blow up?
¿Sabe cuándo va a explotar?
¿SAH-beh KWAHN-doh vah ah ehx-ploh-TAHR?

When?
¿Cuándo?
¿KWAHN-doh?

Where did you make the bomb?
¿Dónde hizo la bomba?
¿DOHN-deh EE-soh lah BOHM-bah?

Are there any other bombs?
¿Hay otras bombas?
¿ai OH-trahs BOHM-bahs?

Where?
¿Dónde?
¿DOHN-deh?

Crowd Control

There's not a lot to discuss for crowd control. The goal is to move people away from the target location, for everyone's safety.

Everyone needs to get back!
¡Todos, atrás!
¡TOH-dohs, ah-TRAHS!

Everyone needs to remain calm!
¡Manténganse todos en calma!
¡mahn-TEHN-gahn-seh TOH-dohs ehn KAHL-mah!

Large Disasters

Whether it's a man-made disaster or a natural disaster, the following commands will be helpful.

We are evacuating the area. Everyone must leave.

Estamos evacuando el área. Todo el mundo tiene que irse.

ehs-TAH-mohs eh-vah-koo-AHN-doh ehl AH-reh-ah.
TOH-doh ehl MOON-doh tee-EH-neh keh EER-seh.

Leave as quickly and safely as possible.

Váyase rápido y con cuidado tan pronto como pueda.

VAH-yah-seh RAH-pee-doh ee kohn koo-ee-DAH-doh
tahn PROHN-toh KOH-moh PWEH-dah.

Do not return to your home until instructed to do so.

No regrese a su casa hasta que se le dé instrucciones de hacerlo.

noh reh-GREH-seh ah soo KAH-sah AHS-tah keh seh
leh deh een-strook-see-OH-nehs deh ah-SEHR-loh.

Go inside your homes, into the most secure area of the house, and wait for further instructions.

Entren a sus casas, en las áreas más seguras de la casa, y esperen que le demos instrucciones.

EHN-trehn ah soos KAH-sahs, ehn lahs AH-reh-ahs
MAHS seh-GOO-rahs deh lah KAH-sah, ee ehs-PEH-
rehn keh leh DEH-mohs een-strook-see-OH-nehs.

Do not touch the downed power line.

No toquen los cables de electricidad.

noh TOH-kehn lohs KAH-blehs deh eh-lehk-tree-see-
DAHD.

Lie down on the floor until we can get you help.
Acuéstense en el piso hasta que los podamos ayudar.
ah-coo-EHS-teh-seh ehn ehl PEE-soh AHS-tah keh lohs poh-DAH-mohs ah-yoo-DAHR.

Helpful Phrases

Here are some final phrases to help you handle the situations this chapter covered.

Be patient with me, please; I speak only a little Spanish.
Tenga paciencia conmigo, por favor; hablo sola-mente un poquito de español.
TEHN-gah pah-see-EHN-see-ah kohn-MEE-goh, pohr fah-VOHR; AH-bloh soh-lah-MEHN-teh oon poh-KEE-toh deh ehs-pah-NYOHL.

We are waiting for a fluent Spanish speaker.
Estamos esperando a una persona que habla español.
ehs-TAH-mohs ehs-peh-RAHN-doh ah OO-nah pehr-SOH-nah keh AH-blah ehs-pah-NYOHL.

We are trying to make sure everyone goes home safely.
Estamos tratando de que todos lleguen a sus casas a salvo.
ehs-TAH-mohs trah-TAHN-doh deh keh TOH-dohs YEH-gehn ah soos KAH-sahs ah SAHL-voh.

Community Policing

In This Chapter

- Creating block watches
- Dealing with disturbances
- Handling neighbor disputes and unsightly properties
- Criminal abatement proceedings

Community policing involves helping the people in your community improve their neighborhoods and quality of living. The phrases in this chapter help you respond to everything from loud music to neighbor disputes.

Community Events

Police departments often assist with organizing community events, as well as participate in them. These include block watch organizations and parties.

Do you have a block watch organization in your neighborhood?

¿Tiene una organización de "vigilancia comunitaria" en su vecindario?

*¿tee-EH-neh OO-nah ohr-gah-nee-sah-see-OHN deh
"vee-hee-LAHN-see-ah koh-moo-nee-TAH-ree-ah" ehn
soo veh-seen-DAH-ree-oh?*

Are you interested in heading a block watch group?

¿Está usted interesado en encabezar un grupo de
vigilancia comunitaria?

*¿ehs-TAH oo-STEHD een-teh-rehs-AH-doh ehn ehn-
kah-beh-SAHR oon GROO-poh de vee-hee-LAHN-see-
ah koh-moo-nee-TAH-ree-ah?*

This would require education/training from the police department.

Esto requiere recibir educación y entrenamiento
por parte del departamento de policía.

*EHS-toh reh-KEE-eh-reh reh-see-BEER eh-doo-kah-
see-OHN ee ehn-treh-nah-mee-EHN-toh pohr PAHR-
teh dehl deh-pahr-tah-MEHN-toh deh poh-lee-SEE-ah.*

It would require regular meetings.

Requiere asistir a reuniones regularmente.

*reh-KEE-eh-reh ah-sees-TEER ah reh-oo-nee-OH-nehs
reh-goo-lahr-MEHN-teh.*

It would allow communication among neighbors and a partnership with the police department.

Esto permite la comunicación entre vecindarios y una
relación estrecha con el departamento de policía.

*EHS-toh pehr-MEE-teh lah koh-moo-nee-kah-see-OHN
EHN-treh veh-seen-DAH-ree-ohs ee OO-nah reh-lah-see-
OHN ehs-TREH-chah kohn ehl deh-pahr-tah-MEHN-
toh deh poh-lee-SEE-ah.*

The police department will help you organize the group.

El departamento de policía lo/la va a ayudar a organizar el grupo.

ehl deh-pahr-tah-MEHN-toh de poh-lee-SEE-ah loh/lah vah ah ah-yoo-DAHR ah ohr-gah-nee-SAHR ehl GROO-poh.

A block watch group would help combat crime in your neighborhood.

El grupo de vigilancia comunitaria ayudará a combatir el crimen en su vecindario.

ehl GROO-poh deh vee-hee-LAHN-see-ah koh-moo-nee-TAH-ree-ah ah-yoo-dah-RAH ah kohm-bah-TEER ehl KREE-mehn ehn soo veh-seen-DAH-ree-oh.

Often there are no exact translations for specific English words. If that's the case, give an explanation of the word instead.

Loud Music

Loud music and parties are a large problem in some neighborhoods. Being able to communicate to the people disrupting the neighborhood is paramount to solving the problem.

Turn the music off, please.

Apague la música, por favor.

ah-PAH-geh lah MOO-see-kah, pohr fah-VOHR.

Is this your house?
¿Es ésta su casa?
¿ehs EHS-tah soo KAH-sah?

Do you own it or rent it?
¿Es usted el dueño/la dueña o el inquilino/
la inquilina?
*¿ehs oo-STEHD ehl doo-EH-nyoh/lah doo-EH-nyah oh
ehl een-kee-LEE-noh/la een-kee-LEE-nah?*

You need to keep your music turned down.
Usted necesita mantener el volumen de la música
bajo.
*oo-STEHD neh-seh-SEE-tah mahn-teh-NEHR ehl
voh-LOO-mehn deh lah MOO-see-kah BAH-hoh.*

You need to keep your music off.
Usted debe mantener la música apagada.
*oo-STEHD DEH-beh mahn-teh-NEHR lah MOO-see-
kah ah-pah-GAH-dah.*

**We are receiving complaints from your neigh-
bors about the music being too loud.**
Recibimos quejas de sus vecinos de que la música
está demasiado alta.
*reh-see-BEE-mohs KEH-hahs deh soos veh-SEE-nohs
deh keh lah MOO-see-kah ehs-TAH deh-mah-see-AH-
doh AHL-tah.*

The music was too loud.
La música está muy alta.
lah MOO-see-kah ehs-TAH MOO-ee AHL-tah.

I am giving you a ticket for disturbing the neighborhood.

Le voy a dar una multa por molestar a su vecindario.

leh voi ah dahr OO-nah MOOL-tah pohr moh-lehs-TAHR ah soo veh-seen-DAH-ree-oh.

If you turn your music back on, we will return and write you a ticket.

Si vuelve a poner la música, vamos a volver para darle una multa.

see voo-EHL-veh ah poh-NEHR lah MOO-see-kah, VAH-mohs ah vohl-VEHR PAH-rah DAHR-leh OO-nah MOOL-tah.

Neighbor Disputes

Neighbor disputes are some of the most frustrating calls police officers respond to. There's seldom an immediate solution, and they usually require ongoing work with the parties involved.

How long have you lived in this house?

¿Hace cuánto tiempo que vive en esta casa?

¿AH-seh KWAHN-toh tee-EHM-poh keh VEE-veh ehn EHS-tah KAH-sah?

Where are your property lines?

¿Dónde están los límites de su propiedad?

¿DOHN-deh ehs-TAHN lohs LEE-mee-tehs deh soo proh-pee-eh-DAHD?

How long has your neighbor lived in his/her house?
¿Hace cuánto tiempo que su vecino vive en la casa?
¿AH-seh KWAHN-toh tee-EHM-poh keh soo veh-SEE-noh VEE-veh ehn lah KAH-sah?

Is this an ongoing problem?
¿Este es un problema constante?
¿EHS-teh ehs oon proh-BLEH-mah kohn-STAHN-teh?

How long have you had problems with your neighbor?
¿Hace cuánto tiempo que tiene problemas con su vecino?
¿AH-seh KWAHN-toh tee-EHM-poh tee-EH-neh proh-BLEH-mahs kohn soo veh-SEE-noh?

Have you attempted mediation with your neighbor?
¿Ha tratado de mediar oficialmente con su vecino?
¿ah trah-TAH-doh deh meh-dee-AHR oh-fee-see-ahl-MEHN-teh kohn soo veh-SEE-noh?

If we set up mediation proceedings, would you be willing to participate?
Si establecemos un proceso formal de mediación, ¿usted estaría dispuesto/a a participar?
see ehs-tah-bleh-SEH-mohs oon proh-SEH-soh fohr-MAHL deh meh-dee-ah-see-OHN, ¿oo-STEHD ehs-tah-REE-ah dees-PWEHS-toh/tah ah pahr-tee-see-PAHR?

Unclean Property

Police departments sometimes respond to complaints of properties whose appearances are offensive to the neighborhood. Most police departments work with the owners of the property or other city services to clean up the property.

Do you own this house?
¿Usted es el dueño/la dueña de esta casa?
¿oo-STEHD ehs ehl DWEH-nyoh/nyah deh EHS-tah KAH-sah?

Who is the owner?
¿Quién es el dueño/a?
¿kee-EHN ehs ehl DWEH-nyoh/nyah?

How do I contact the owner?
¿Cómo puedo contactar al dueño/a la dueña?
¿KOH-moh PWEH-doh kohn-tahk-TAHR ahl DWEH-nyoh/ah lah DWEH-nyah?

The trash on this property is unacceptable.
La basura en esta propiedad es inaceptable.
lah bah-SOO-rah ehn EHS-tah proh-pee-eh-DAHD ehs een-ah-sehp-TAH-bleh.

The weeds on this property are unacceptable.
Las hierbas/los cardos en esta propiedad son inaceptables.
lahs ee-EHR-bahs/lohs KAHR-dohs ehn EHS-tah proh-pee-eh-DAHD sohn een-ah-sehp-TAH-blehs.

You have to clean up your property.
Tiene que limpiar su propiedad.
tee-EH-neh keh leem-pee-AHR soo proh-pee-eh-DAHD.

You have _____ days/weeks/months to clean the property.
Usted tiene _____ días/semanas/meses para limpiar esta propiedad.
oo-STEHD tee-EH-neh _____ DEE-ahs/seh-MAH-nahs/MEH-sehs PAH-rah leem-pee-AHR EHS-tah proh-pee-eh-DAHD.

Criminal Abatement

Some states allow police departments to abate, or take possession of, property that's allowing criminal activity to occur there or where ongoing criminal activity is occurring.

How long have you owned this property?
¿Hace cuánto tiempo que es el dueño/la dueña de esta propiedad?
¿AH-seh KWAHN-toh tee-EHM-poh ehs ehl DWEH-nyoh/lah DWEH-nyah deh EHS-tah proh-pee-eh-DAHD?

Do you own it outright, or are you still paying it off?
¿La casa está pagada, o todavía está pagándola por mes?
¿lah KAH-sah ehs-TAH pah-GAH-dah, oh toh-dah-VEE-ah ehs-TAH pah-GAHN-doh-lah pohr mehs?

Are you aware of the criminal activity occurring on your property?

¿Usted sabe acerca de las actividades criminales que pasan en su propiedad?

¿oo-STEHD SAH-beh ah-SEHR-kah deh lahs ahk-tee-vee-DAH-dehs kree-mee-NAH-lehs keh PAH-sahn ehn soo proh-pee-eh-DAHD?

Did you receive the letter we sent advising you of the activity on your property?

¿Recibió usted la carta que le mandamos indicán-dole acerca de la actividad en su propiedad?

¿reh-see-bee-OH oo-STEHD lah KAHR-tah keh leh mahn-DAH-mohs een-dee-KAHN-doh-leh ah-SEHR-kah deh lah ahk-tee-vee-DAHD ehn soo proh-pee-eh-DAHD?

Do you understand that if you do not clean up your property, we are going to take possession of it?

¿Comprende usted que si no limpia su propiedad vamos a tomar posesión de ella?

¿kohm-PREHN-deh oo-STEHD keh see noh LEEM-pee-ah soo proh-pee-eh-DAHD VAH-mohs ah toh-MAHR poh-seh-see-OHN deh eyah?

Helpful Phrases

Because community policing requires that the police work hand in hand with the neighborhood, here are some phrases that will help the relationship.

We want to help you have a safer neighborhood.
Queremos ayudarlo/la a tener un vecindario seguro.
keh-REH-mohs ah-yoo-DAHR-loh/lah ah teh-NEHR
oon veh-seen-DAH-ree-oh seh-GOO-roh.

**We need your help to clean up the neighbor-
hood.**
Necesitamos su ayuda para limpiar el vecindario.
neh-seh-see-TAH-mohs soo ah-YOO-dah PAH-rah
leem-pee-AHR ehl veh-seen-DAH-ree-oh.

**A safe neighborhood is a partnership between
police and the neighborhood. We cannot do it
alone.**
Un vecindario seguro depende en parte de una relación estrecha entre la policía y el vecindario. No lo
podemos hacer nosotros solos.
oon veh-seen-DAH-ree-oh seh-GOO-roh deh-PEHN-
deh ehn PAHR-teh deh OO-nah reh-lah-see-OHN
ehs-TREH-chah EHN-treh lah poh-lee-SEE-ah ee ehl
veh-seen-DAH-ree-oh. noh loh poh-DEH-mohs ah-
SEHR noh-SOH-trohs SOH-lohs.

12

Making the Arrest

In This Chapter

- High-risk commands for kneeling and standing suspects
- High-risk stop commands for suspects in vehicles
- Miranda warnings

Arrests can be both high risk and low risk, depending on the circumstances. The commands in this chapter enable you to take someone into custody in all conceivable situations.

High-Risk Commands

During high-risk situations, law enforcement need to be able to give commands to take the suspect into custody safely. These commands are probably the most important part of this book, and can be used to save the lives of law enforcement officers, civilians, and suspects.

Arresting a Standing Suspect

_____ **Police Department!**
¡Departamento de Policía de _____!
¡deh-pahr-tah-MEHN-toh deh poh-lee-SEE-ah deh
_____!

Do not move.
No se mueva.
noh seh moo-EH-vah.

Turn around.
Voltéese.
vohl-TEH-eh-seh.

Stop.
Alto.
AHL-toh.

Walk backward toward me.
Camine para atrás hacia mí.
kah-MEE-neh PAH-rah ah-TRAHS ah-see-ah MEE.

Prior to having the suspect walk backward to you, always stop them facing away from you.

Separate your feet.
Separe los pies.
seh-PAH-reh lohs pee-EHS.

Hands on your head.
Manos en la cabeza.
MAH-nohs ehn lah kah-BEH-sah.

Arresting a Kneeling Suspect

If you encounter a suspect who's kneeling, here's how to handle the arrest.

The phrases "¡Departamento de Policía de _____ !" and "No se mueva" are appropriate here. However, rather than continuing to repeat phrases throughout this chapter, know that you need to say certain phrases for safety or clarification throughout the command phrases.

Turn around.
Voltéese.
vohl-TEH-eh-seh.

Stop.
Alto.
AHL-toh.

Lift your shirt. Slowly.
Levante la camisa. Despacio.
leh-VAHN-teh lah kah-MEE-sah. deh-SPAH-see-oh.

Turn around. Slowly.
Voltéese. Despacio.
vohl-TEH-eh-seh. deh-SPAH-see-oh.

Walk backward toward me.
Camine para atrás hacia mí.
kah-MEE-neh PAH-rah ah-TRAHS AH-see-ah MEE.

On your knees.
De rodillas.
deh roh-DEE-yahs.

Cross your feet.
Cruce los pies.
KROO-seh lohs pee-EHS.

Hands on your head.
Manos en la cabeza.
MAH-nohs ehn lah kah-BEH-sah.

You are under arrest.
Está arrestado/a.
ehs-TAH ahr-rehs-TAH-doh/dah.

Arresting a Standing Suspect

If you encounter a suspect who's standing, here's how to handle the arrest.

Walk backward toward me.
Camine para atrás hacia mí.
kah-MEE-neh PAH-rah ah-TRAHS ah-SEE-ah MEE.

Do not look at me.
No me mire.
noh meh MEE-reh.

Do not talk.
No hable.
noh AH-bleh.

On your knees.
De rodillas.
deh roh-DEE-yahs.

Lie down mouth down.
Acuéstese boca abajo.
ah-coo-EHS-teh-seh BOH-kah ah-BAH-hoh.

The phrase *boca abajo* is an idiomatic phrase and means the same as "face down" to English speakers.

Hands on your back.
Manos en la espalda.
MAH-nohs ehn lah eh-SPAHL-dah.

Arresting Suspect(s) in a Vehicle

When you're dealing with suspects who are still in their car, use these phrases.

Everyone, hands up!
¡Todos, manos arriba!
¡TOH-dohs, MAH-nohs ahr-REE-bah!

Or:

Everyone, hands on your head!
¡Todos, manos en la cabeza!
¡TOH-dohs, MAH-nohs ehn lah kah-BEH-sah!

Do not move!
¡No se muevan!
¡noh seh moo-EH-vahn!

Driver, turn off the motor!
¡Conductor, apague el motor!
¡kohn-dook-TOHR, ah-PAH-geh ehl moh-TOHR!

Throw the keys out the window.
Tire las llaves por la ventana.
TEE-reh lahs YAH-vehs pohr lah vehn-TAH-nah.

Put the keys out the window and drop them.
Ponga las llaves afuera de la ventana y suéltelas.
*POHN-gah lahs YAH-vehs ah-foo-EH-rah deh lah
vehn-TAH-nah ee soo-EHL-teh-lahs.*

Or:

Keys out.
Llaves afuera.
YAH-vehs ah-foo-EH-rah.

Drop them.
Suéltelas.
soo-EHL-teh-lahs.

Driver, open the door.
Conductor, abra la puerta.
kohn-dook-TOHR, AH-brah lah PWEHR-tah.

Driver, get out of the car.
Conductor, salga del carro.
kohn-dook-TOHR, SAHL-gah dehl KAHR-roh.

Or:

Driver, get out of the car.
Conductor, bájese del carro.
kohn-dook-TOHR, BAH-heh-seh dehl KAHR-roh.

Driver, return to the car.
Conductor, regrese al carro.
kohn-DOOK-tohr, reh-GREH-seh ahl KAHR-roh.

Or:

Driver, get back in the car.
Conductor, súbase al carro.
kohn-dook-TOHR, SOO-bah-seh ahl KAHR-roh.

Hands up!
¡Manos arriba!
¡MAH-nohs ahr-REE-bah!

Lift your shirt.
Levantese la camisa.
leh-VAHN-teh-seh lah kah-MEE-sah.

Turn around!
¡Voltéese!
¡vohl-TEH-eh-seh!

Walk backward toward me.
Camine para atrás hacia mí.
kah-MEE-neh PAH-rah ah-TRAHS AH-see-ah MEE.

One step to your right/left.
Un paso a su derecha/izquierda.
oon PAH-soh ah soo deh-REH-chah/ees-kee-EHR-dah.

Continue!
¡Siga!
¡SEE-gah!

Throw yourself onto the ground.
Tírese al suelo.
TEE-reh-seh ahl soo-EH-loh.

The phrase *Tírese al suelo* is also an idiomatic phrase commonly used to order subjects onto the ground. The literal translation is "throw yourself onto the ground" but means "put yourself on the ground."

On your knees. Cross your feet.
De rodillas. Cruce los pies.
deh roh-DEE-yahs. KROO-seh lohs pee-EHS.

Front passenger
Pasajero del frente
pah-sah-HEH-roh dehl FREHN-teh

After identifying that you are talking to the front seat passenger, repeat the command phrases to call the front passenger(s) out of the vehicle.

Back passenger, left side *Or:* **right side**
Pasajero de atrás, lado izquierdo *Or:* lado derecho
pah-sah-HEH-roh deh ah-TRAHS, LAH-doh ees-kee-EHR-doh Or: *LAH-doh deh-REH-choh*

One back passenger
Un pasajero de atrás
oon pah-sah-HEH-roh deh ah-TRAHS

Placing Suspects Under Arrest

Ideally, placing handcuffs on someone will be easy, and then all you have to do is advise him/her that he/she is under arrest.

You are under arrest.
Está arrestado/a.
ehs-TAH ahr-rehs-TAH-doh/ah.

Helpful Arrest Commands

English	Spanish	Pronunciation
do not talk	no hable	*noh AH-bleh*
get out	salga	*SAHL-gah*
move	muévase	*moo-EH-vah-seh*
shut up	cállese	*KAH-yeh-seh*
silence	silencio	*see-lehn-SEE-oh*
sit down	siéntese	*see-EHN-teh-seh*
stand up	levántese	*leh-VAHN-teh-seh*

I am going to search you.
Lo voy a esculcar.
loh voi ah ehs-kool-KAHR.

Do you have anything in your pockets?
¿Tiene algo en sus bolsillos?
¿tee-EH-neh AHL-goh ehn soos bohl-SEE-yohs?

Miranda Warnings

When someone has been arrested, language barrier or not, and law enforcement intends on questioning the suspect, the suspect needs to know when Miranda applies.

You have the right to remain silent.
Usted tiene el derecho de guardar silencio.
oo-STEHD tee-EH-neh ehl deh-REH-choh deh goo-ahr-DAHR see-LEHN-see-oh.

Anything you say can be used against you in a court of law.
Cualquier cosa que diga se puede usar en su contra en los tribunales de justicia.
kwahl-kee-EHR KOH-sah keh DEE-gah seh poo-EH-deh oo-SAHR ehn soo KOHN-trah ehn lohs tree-boo-NAH-lehs deh hoo-STEE-see-ah.

You have the right to have an attorney present before and during questioning if you so desire.
Usted tiene el derecho de tener un abogado presente antes y durante las preguntas si usted lo desea.
oo-STEHD tee-EH-neh ehl deh-REH-choh deh teh-NEHR oon ah-boh-GAH-doh preh-SEHN-teh AHN-tehs ee doo-RAHN-teh lahs preh-GOON-tahs see oo-STEHD loh deh-SEH-ah.

If you cannot afford an attorney, you have the right to have an attorney appointed for you prior to questioning.

Si usted no tiene los fondos para pagar un abogado, usted tiene el derecho a que el tribunal le nombre a uno para que le asista antes de comenzar con las preguntas.

see oo-STEHD noh tee-EH-neh lohs FOHN-dohs PAH-rah pah-GAHR oon ah-boh-GAH-doh, OO-stehd tee-EH-neh ehl deh-REH-choh ah keh ehl tree-boo-NAHL leh NOHM-breh ah OO-noh PAH-rah keh leh ah-SEES-tah AHN-tehs deh koh-mehn-SAHR kohn lahs preh-GOON-tahs.

Do you understand these rights? Yes or no?

¿Comprende usted estos derechos? ¿Sí o no?

¿kohm-PREHN-deh oo-STEHD EHS-tohs deh-REH-chohs? ¿see oh noh?

Helpful Phrases

Making an arrest can be a stressful and suspenseful situation. Keep your head, and use these phrases to get through it safely.

I see the weapon. Do not touch it.

Veo el arma. No la toque.

VEH-oh ehl AHR-mah. noh lah TOH-keh.

Put the weapon on the floor.

Ponga el arma en el suelo.

POHN-gah ehl AHR-mah ehn ehl soo-EH-loh.

Drop it!
¡Suéltela!
¡soo-EHL-teh-lah!

Do not talk. (plural)
No hablen.
noh AH-blehn.

Or:

Do not talk. (singular)
No hable.
noh AH-bleh.

13

At the Detention Facility

In This Chapter

- Intake phrases
- Phrases for fingerprinting
- Booking searches
- Combative prisoners
- Safety in the cells

The following words and phrases will be useful after the arrestee has reached the detention facility. The phrases enable you to obtain necessary information and conduct searches specific to detention facilities.

Intake Questions

The following basic questions allow law enforcement to obtain pertinent information for the intake process.

What is your birthday?
¿Cuándo es su fecha de nacimiento/día de cumpleaños?
¿KWAHN-doh ehs soo FEH-chah deh nah-see-mee-EHN-toh/DEE-ah deh koom-plee-AH-nyohs?

Are you thinking about committing suicide?
¿Está pensado en suicidarse?
¿ehs-TAH pehn-SAHN-doh ehn soo-ee-see-DAHR-seh?

Have you ever been suicidal?
¿Alguna vez pensó en suicidarse?
¿ahl-GOO-nah vehs pehn-SOH ehn soo-ee-see-DAHR-seh?

Are you thinking about hurting yourself?
¿Piensa lastimarse?
¿pee-EHN-sah lahs-tee-MAHR-seh?

Are you affiliated with any gangs?
¿Está usted afiliado a alguna pandilla?
¿ehs-TAH oo-STEHD ah-fee-lee-AH-doh ah ahl-GOO-nah pahn-DEE-yah?

> **Street Slang**
> If the subject does not understand the word *pandilla* (*pahn-DEE-yah*), use the word *ganga* (*GAHN-gah*); it is very common street slang for "gang."

I need to take your picture.
Necesito tomarle una foto.
neh-seh-SEE-toh toh-MAHR-leh OO-nah FOH-toh.

Fingerprinting

Regardless of the location where they're taken, be it a precinct or the detention facility, a suspect's fingerprints are always taken if they're getting booked. The following phrases make the process a little easier.

We are going to take your fingerprints.
Vamos a tomar sus huellas digitales.
VAH-mohs ah toh-MAHR soos oo-EH-yahs dee-hee-TAHL-ehs.

Give me your right/left hand.
Deme su mano derecha/izquierda.
DEH-meh soo MAH-noh deh-REH-chah/ees-kee-EHR-dah.

Relax your hand.
Relaje su mano.
reh-LAH-heh soo MAH-noh.

Give me this finger and straighten it.
Deme este dedo y póngalo derecho.
DEH-meh EHS-teh DEH-doh ee POHN-gah-loh deh-REH-choh.

Relax your finger.
Relaje su dedo.
reh-LAH-heh soo DEH-doh.

Allow me to roll your finger.
Deje que ruede su dedo.
DEH-heh keh roo-EH-deh soo DEH-doh.

Booking Searches

Suspects are normally searched after they reach intake. The following commands assist with those searches.

Do you have any knives, needles, or drugs on you?
¿Tiene algún cuchillo, agujas, o drogas con usted?
¿tee-EH-neh ahl-GOON koo-CHEE-yoh, ah-GOO-hahs, oh DROH-gahs kohn oo-STEHD?

 Although subjects are always searched, there are the unfortunate occasions when items are missed during the original search.

If you do have any items of contraband on your person, you will be charged with a felony.
Si tiene algún objeto de contrabando con usted, usted será acusado de un delito mayor/grave.
see tee-EH-neh ahl-GOON ohh-HEH-toh deh kohn-trah-BAHN-doh kohn oo-STEHD, oo-STEHD seh-RAH ah-koo-SAH-doh deh oon deh-LEE-toh mah-YOHR/GRAH-veh.

Spread your feet, please.
Separe los pies, por favor.
seh-PAH-reh lohs pee-EHS, pohr fah-VOHR.

Turn around; lift one foot up at a time.
Dese vuelta; levante un pie a la vez.
DEH-seh voo-EHL-tah; leh-VAHN-teh oon pee-EH ah lah vehs.

Take each piece of clothing off and hand it to me.
Quítese cada prenda de ropa y démela.
KEE-teh-seh KAH-dah PREHN-dah deh ROH-pah ee DEH-meh-lah.

Open your mouth. Lift your tongue. Run your fingers along your gums.
Abra su boca. Levante la lengua. Toque sus encías con sus dedos.
AH-brah soo BOH-kah. leh-VAHN-teh lah LEHN-gwah. TOH-keh soos ehn-SEE-ahs kohn soos DEH-dohs.

Let me see inside your ears. Behind your ears.
Déjeme ver adentro de sus orejas. Atrás de sus orejas.
DEH-heh-meh vehr ah-DEHN-troh deh soos oh-REH-hahs. ah-TRAHS deh soos oh-REH-hahs.

When the handcuffs are removed, place your hands on top of your head.
Cuando le saque las esposas, ponga sus manos arriba de su cabeza.
KWAHN-doh leh SAH-keh lahs ehs-POH-sahs, POHN-gah soos MAH-nohs ahr-REE-bah deh soo kah-BEH-sah.

Strip Searches for Females

Certain commands are specific to female searches.

Reach your hands toward the ceiling.
Extienda sus manos hacia el techo.
ehx-tee-EHN-dah soos MAH-nohs AH-see-ah ehl TEH-choh.

Lift each breast, one at a time.
Levante cada seno, uno a la vez.
leh-VAHN-teh KAH-dah SEH-noh, OO-noh ah lah vehs.

Squat down to the ground; cough hard three times.
Póngase en cuclillas; tosa fuerte tres veces.
POHN-gah-seh ehn kook-LEE-yahs; TOH-sah foo-EHR-teh trehs VEH-sehs.

Stand up, still facing that wall, bend over, spread your buttocks and vagina, cough hard three times.
Levántese, todavía mirando hacia la pared, agáchese, sepárese las nalgas y la vagina, tosa tres veces.
leh-VAHN-teh-seh, toh-dah-VEE-ah mee-RAHN-doh AH-see-ah lah pah-REHD, ah-GAH-cheh-seh ee seh-PAH-reh-seh lahs NAHL-gahs ee lah vah-HEE-nah, TOH-sah trehs VEH-sehs.

Get dressed, please.
Vístase, por favor.
VEES-tah-seh, pohr fah-VOHR.

Combative Prisoners

Certain commands are necessary for subjects who are not cooperative with law enforcement. The following commands will serve to be very useful in such situations.

Do not resist.
No se resista.
noh seh reh-SEES-tah.

Stop resisting.
Deje de resistirse.
DEH-heh deh reh-sees-TEER-seh.

Give me your hands.
Deme sus manos.
DEH-meh soos MAH-nohs.

Give me your legs.
Deme sus piernas.
DEH-meh SOOS pee-EHR-nahs.

Go down to your knees.
Póngase de rodillas.
POHN-gah-seh deh roh-DEE-yahs.

Get down on the ground.
Tírese al suelo.
TEE-reh-seh ahl soo-EH-loh.

Lie down on the ground on your stomach.
Acuéstese en el suelo, panza abajo.
ah-koo-EHS-teh-seh ehn ehl soo-EH-loh, PAHN-sah ah-BAH-hoh.

Cross your feet.
Cruce los pies.
KROO-seh lohs pee-EHS.

Drop what is in your hands.
Suelte lo que tiene en las manos.
soo-EHL-teh loh keh tee-EH-neh ehn lahs MAH-nohs.

Hands behind your back.
Manos atrás de su espalda.
MAH-nohs ah-TRAHS deh soo ehs-PAHL-dah.

Place your hands on top of your head.
Ponga sus manos arriba de su cabeza.
POHN-gah soos MAH-nohs ahr-REE-bah deh soo kah-BEH-sah.

Interlace your fingers.
Cruce los dedos.
KROO-seh lohs DEH-dohs.

Safety in the Cells

The following enable you to deliver important commands to the prisoner while he/she is in his/her cell.

Close the door.
Cierre la puerta.
see-EHR-reh lah poo-EHR-tah.

Sit down.
Siéntese
see-EHN-teh-seh.

Will you comply by taking your clothes off by yourself?
¿Va a colaborar quitandose la ropa usted solo?
¿vah ah koh-lah-boh-RAHR kee-TAHN-doh-seh lah ROH-pah oo-STEHD SOH-loh?

Do not move until you hear the door close.
No se mueva hasta que escuche que la puerta se cerró.
noh seh moo-EH-vah ahs-TAH keh ehs-KOO-cheh keh lah poo-EHR-tah seh sehr-ROH.

What is your emergency?
¿Cuál es su emergencia?
¿KWAHL ehs soo eh-mehr-HEHN-see-ah?

Sit down on your bed.
Siéntese en su cama.
see-EHN-teh-seh ehn soo KAH-mah.

Place your hands behind your back.
Ponga sus manos detrás de su espalda.
POHN-gah soos MAH-nohs deh-TRAHS deh soo ehs-PAHL-dah.

Do you feel like hurting yourself?
¿Tiene ganas de lastimarse?
¿tee-EH-neh GAH-nahs deh lah-stee-MAHR-seh?

Helpful Phrases

The following general phrases and commands will assist with controlling prisoners.

Go to your cell.
Vaya a su celda.
VAH-yah a soo SEHL-dah.

Wash your hands.
Lávese las manos.
LAH-veh-seh lahs MAH-nohs.

Dry your hands.
Séquese las manos.
SEH-keh-seh lahs MAH-nohs.

Stand there. Don't move.
Párese allí. No se mueva.
PAH-reh-seh ah-YEE. noh seh moo-EH-vah.

Are you having an emergency?
¿Tiene una emergencia?
¿tee-EH-neh OO-nah eh-mehr-HEHN-see-ah?

Lock down. Return to bunk.
Cierre de celda. Regrese a su cama.
see-EHR-reh deh SEHL-dah. reh-GREH-seh ah soo KAH-mah.

Keep the noise down.
No haga ruido.
noh AH-gah roo-EE-doh.

Post-Crime Proceedings

In This Chapter

- Questions upon release
- Probation regulations
- Behavior regulations

Certain information is needed prior to releasing a defendant from custody. Likewise, certain agreements need to be made before releasing the inmate into the probation system.

Questions upon Release

The following questions enable the courts, probation officers, and/or the detention institution to obtain pertinent information needed upon an inmate's release.

Your legal name?
¿Su nombre legal?
¿soo NOHM-breh leh-GAHL?

How long have you been living at your residence?

¿Cuánto tiempo tiene viviendo en su domicilio?

¿KWAHN-toh tee-EHM-poh tee-EH-neh vee-vee-EHN-doh ehn soo doh-mee-SEE-lee-oh?

Where were you born? (city, state, and country)

¿Lugar de nacimiento? (ciudad, estado, y país)

¿loo-GAHR deh nah-see-mee-EHN-toh? (see-oo-DAHD, ehs-TAH-doh, ee pah-EES)

Have you ever been deported?

¿Ha sido deportado alguna vez?

¿ah SEE-doh deh-pohr-TAH-doh ahl-GOO-nah vehs?

Tell me all the cities and states you have lived in.

Dígame todas las ciudades y estados en los que ha vivido.

DEE-gah-meh TOH-dahs lahs see-oo-DAH-dehs ee ehs-TAH-dohs ehn lohs keh ah vee-VEE-doh.

Your father's complete name?

¿Nombre completo de su padre?

¿NOHM-breh kohm-PLEH-toh deh soo PAH-dreh?

Your mother's complete name?

¿Nombre completo de su madre?

¿NOHM-breh kohm-PLEH-toh deh soo MAH-dreh?

Civil status?

¿Estado civil?

¿ehs-TAH-doh see-VEEL?

How many children do you have?

¿Cuántos niños tiene?

¿KWAHN-tohs NEE-nyohs tee-EH-neh?

Who do you live with?
¿Con quién vive?
¿kohn kee-EHN VEE-veh?

Are they with you?
¿Están ellos con usted?
¿ehs-TAHN EH-yohs kohn oo-STEHD?

Have your children ever been taken by the state into protective custody?
¿Alguna vez el estado le sacó a sus hijos y los puso bajo custodia?
¿ahl-GOO-nah vehs ehl ehs-TAH-doh leh sah-KOH ah soos EE-hohs ee lohs POO-soh BAH-hoh koos-TOH-dee-ah?

If they have, when and why?
Si es así, ¿cuándo y por qué?
see ehs ah-SEE, ¿KWAHN-doh ee pohr KEH?

Do you have mental health problems?
¿Tiene problemas de salud mental?
¿tee-EH-neh proh-BLEH-mahs deh sah-LOOD mehn-TAHL?

Are you taking medication?
¿Está tomando medicamentos?
¿ehs-TAH toh-MAHN-doh meh-dee-kah-MEHN-tohs?

How many years of school did you complete?
¿Años de escuela que terminó?
¿AH-nyohs deh ehs-koo-EH-lah keh tehr-mee-NOH?

Name of your employer?
¿Nombre del empleador?
¿NOHM-breh dehl ehm-pleh-ah-DOHR?

The date you started?
¿Fecha que empezó?
¿FEH-chah keh ehm-peh-SOH?

Name and telephone number of your supervisor?
¿Nombre y teléfono de su supervisor?
¿NOHM-breh ee teh-LEH-foh-noh deh soo soo-pehr-vee-SOHR?

What is your salary?
¿Cuál es su salario?
¿KWAHL ehs soo sah-LAH-ree-oh?

If you are unemployed, how long have you been unemployed?
Si está desempleado, ¿hace cuánto?
see ehs-TAH deh-sehm-pleh-AH-doh, ¿AH-seh KWAHN-toh?

How do you support yourself?
¿Cómo se mantiene?
¿KOH-moh seh mahn-tee-EH-neh?

What crime did you commit in order to get arrested?
¿Cuál delito cometió usted para que lo arrestaran?
¿KWAHL deh-LEE-toh koh-meh-tee-OH oo-STEHD PAH-rah keh loh ahr-rehs-TAH-rahn?

Were there victims of this offense?
¿Hubo víctimas en esta ofensa?
¿OO-boh VEEK-tee-mahs ehn EHS-tah oh-FEHN-sah?

Did you injure the victims?
¿Lastimó a las víctimas?
¿lahs-tee-MOH ah lahs VEEK-tee-mahs?

Did you have a weapon in the offense?
¿Portaba un arma en esta offensa?
¿pohr-TAH-bah oon AHR-mah ehn EHS-tah oh-FEHN-sah?

Bote *(BOH-teh)*, gayola *(gah-YOH-lah)*, and *tumba (TOOM-bah)* are common slang terms for "jail," and the phrase *estar en cana (eh-STAHR ehn KAH-nah)* is slang meaning "to be in jail."

What drugs have you consumed, even if it was only one time?
¿Qué drogas ha consumido, aunque haya sido una vez?
¿KEH DROH-gahs ah kohn-soo-MEE-doh, AH-oon-keh AI-yah SEE-doh OO-nah vehs?

Do you think you need treatment for alcohol or drug use?
¿Cree usted que necesita tratamiento por abuso de alcohol o drogas?
¿KREH-eh oo-STEHD keh neh-seh-SEE-tah trah-tah-mee-EHN-toh pohr ah-BOO-soh deh ahl-KOH-hohl oh DROH-gahs?

See the "Types of Drugs" table in Chapter 8 for some common drug terminology.

Probation Regulations

When an inmate is released to probation or parole, certain information is required and certain agreements or understandings must be made.

You must present yourself in person the _____ day of every month between _____ and _____.
Usted tiene que preséntarse en persona el día _____ de cada mes entre las _____ y _____.
oo-STEHD tee-EH-neh keh preh-sehn-TAHR-seh ehn pehr-SOH-nah ehl DEE-ah _____ deh KAH-dah mehs EHN-treh lahs _____ ee _____.

You must submit to a urine or blood test.
Tiene que hacerse un análisis de orina o sangre.
tee-EH-neh keh ah-SEHR-seh oon ah-NAH-lee-sees deh oh-REE-nah oh SAHN-greh.

You must contact the following program by the end of the workday today.
Debe contactar el siguiente programa al final del día de trabajo.
DEH-beh kohn-tahk-TAHR ehl see-gee-EHN-teh proh-GRAH-mah ahl fee-NAHL dehl DEE-ah deh trah-BAH-hoh.

Your participation and completion in the program are a requirement.
Su participación y finalización del programa son un requisito.
soo pahr-tee-see-pah-see-OHN ee fee-nahl-ee-sah-see-OHN dehl proh-GRAH-mah sohn oon reh-kee-SEE-toh.

You must complete _____ hours of community service.
Usted debe completar _____ horas de servicio comunitario.
oo-STEHD DEH-beh kohm-pleh-TAHR _____ OH-rahs deh sehr-VEE-see-oh koh-moo-nee-TAH-ree-oh.

Behavior Regulations

Sometimes you'll need to explain what a person can or cannot do. The following phrases help you do this.

You cannot carry a firearm.
Usted no puede llevar un arma de fuego.
oo-STEHD noh PWEH-deh yeh-VAHR oon AHR-mah deh foo-EH-goh.

You cannot associate with known criminals.
Usted no puede estar relacionado con criminales.
oo-STEHD noh PWEH-deh ehs-TAHR reh-lah-see-oh-NAH-doh kohn kree-mee-NAH-lehs.

You cannot associate with known and documented gang members.

Usted no puede estar relacionado con miembros de pandillas que tenemos registrados.

oo-STEHD noh poo-EH-deh ehs-TAHR reh-lah-see-oh-NAH-doh kohn mee-EHM-brohs deh pahn-DEE-yahs keh teh-NEH-mohs reh-hee-STRAH-dohs.

You cannot contact _____ in person or by electronic communication.

Usted no puede comunicarse con _____ en persona, por teléfono, o por correo electrónico.

oo-STEHD noh PWEH-deh koh-moo-nee-KAHR-seh kohn _____ ehn pehr-SOH-nah, pohr teh-LEH-foh-noh, oh pohr kohr-REH-oh eh-lehk-TROH-nee-koh.

You must cooperate with law enforcement.

Debe cooperar con la policía.

DEH-beh koh-ohpeh-RAHR kohn lah poh-lee-SEE-ah.

You must notify me of any contact with law enforcement.

Usted debe notificarme si tiene contacto con la policía.

oo-STEHD DEH-beh noh-tee-fee-KAHR-meh see tee-EH-neh kohn-TAHK-toh kohn lah poh-lee-SEE-ah.

You cannot travel outside of the state without permission.

Usted no puede viajar afuera del estado sin permiso.

oo-STEHD noh PWEH-deh vee-ah-HAHR ah-foo-EH-rah dehl ehs-TAH-doh seen pehr-MEE-soh.

You cannot travel outside the city limits.
Usted no puede viajar fuera de los límites de la ciudad.
oo-STEHD noh poo-EH-deh vee-ah-HAHR foo-EH-rah deh lohs LEE-mee-tehs deh lah see-oo-DAHD.

Be sure to review these regulations thoroughly and only state the ones pertaining to the current defendant.

If you do not comply with any of the above regulations, your probation rights will be revoked and you will return to jail.
Si no cumple con las reglas citadas, sus derechos de estar bajo prueba se le acabarán y volverá a la cárcel.
see NOH KOOM-pleh kohn lahs REH-glahs see-TAH-dahs, soos deh-REH-chohs deh ehs-TAHR BAH-hoh proo-EH-bah seh leh ah-kah-bah-RAHN ee vohl-veh-RAH ah lah KAHR-sehl.

Helpful Phrases

The following phrases will assist in expediting the release procedures.

Do you understand this regulation?
¿Entiende usted estas reglas?
¿ehn-tee-EHN-deh oo-STEHD EHS-tahs REH-glahs?

Will you comply with this regulation?
¿Va a obedecer estas reglas?
¿vah ah oh-beh-deh-SEHR EHS-tahs REH-glahs?

Call this number if you need immediate help.
Llame a este número si necesita ayuda.
YAH-meh ah EHS-teh NOO-meh-roh see neh-seh-SEE-tah ah-YOO-dah.

We want to make you successful upon your release.
Queremos que usted tenga éxito después de salir de la cárcel.
keh-REH-mohs keh oo-STEHD TEHN-gah EHX-ee-toh dehs-poo-EHS deh sah-LEER deh la KAHR-sehl.

English-to-Spanish Glossary

English	Spanish	Pronunciation
abuse (v)	abusar	ah-boo-SAHR
accident	accidente	ahx-ee-DEHN-teh
accident, vehicle	choque	CHOH-keh
African American/	negro/a	NEH-groh/grah
black/dark skin	moreno/a	moh-REH-noh/nah
	prieto/a	pree-EH-toh/tah
afternoon	en la tarde	ehn lah TAHR-deh
ajudicate	juzgar	HOOS-gahr
AK-47	cuerno de chivo	koo-EHR-noh deh CHEE-voh
alphabet	alfabeto	ahl-fah-BEH-toh
American	americano/a	ah-meh-ree-KAH-noh/nah
amphetamine	anfetamina	ahn-feh-tah-MEE-nah

English	Spanish	Pronunciation
anus	ano	*AH-noh*
Slang:	culo	*KOO-loh*
	cola	*KOH-lah*
	fundillo	*foon-DEE-yoh*
apartment	apartamento	*ah-pahr-tah-MEHN-toh*
April	abril	*AH-breel*
Argentinean	argentino/a	*ahr-hehn-TEE-noh/nah*
arm	brazo	*BRAH-soh*
arrest (v)	arrestar	*ahr-rehs-TAHR*
arrest warrant	orden de arresto	*OHR-dehn deh ahr-REHS-toh*
Asian	asiático/a	*ah-see-AH-tee-koh/kah*
August	agosto	*ah-GOHS-toh*
aunt	tía	*TEE-ah*
automatic rifle	automático/a	*ah-oo-toh-MAH-tee-koh/kah*

continues

continued

English	Spanish	Pronunciation
back	espalda	*ehs-PAHL-dah*
back passenger	pasajero de atrás	*pah-sah-HEH-roh deh ah-TRAHS*
badge	placa	*PLAH-kah*
baker	panadero/a	*pah-nah-DEH-roh/rah*
bakery	panadería	*pah-nah-deh-REE-ah*
bald	pelón	*peh-LOHN*
bank	banco	*BAHN-koh*
baseball hat	cachucha/gorra	*kah-CHOO-chah/GOHR-rah*
bat, baseball	bate	*BAH-teh*
beard	barba	*BAHR-bah*
bike	bicicleta	*bee-see-KLEH-tah*
black (color)	negro	*NEH-groh*
bleed (v)	sangrar	*sahn-GRAHR*

English	Spanish	Pronunciation
block	cuadra	*KWAH-drah*
blood relative	pariente directo	*pah-ree-EHN-teh dee-REHK-toh*
blood	sangre	*SAHN-greh*
blue	azul	*ah-SOOL*
blue, light	celeste	*seh-LEHS-teh*
blue, navy	azul marino	*ah-SOOL mah-REE-noh*
Bolivian	boliviano/a	*boh-lee-vee-AH-noh/nah*
border	la frontera	*lah frohm-TEH-rah*
boss	patrón/jefe	*pah-TROHN/HEH-feh*
boyfriend	novio	*NOH-vee-oh*
braid	trenza	*TREHN-sah*
brake light	luces de freno	*LOO-sehs deh FREH-noh*
brakes	frenos	*FREH-nohs*

continues

continued

English	Spanish	Pronunciation
breast	pecho	*PEH-choh*
Slang:	tetas	*TEH-tahs*
	chichas	*CHEE-chahs*
brick	ladrillo	*lah-DREE-yoh*
brother	hermano	*ehr-MAH-noh*
brother-in-law	cuñado	*koon-YAH-doh*
brown	café/marrón	*kah-FEH/mah-ROHN*
bruise	moreton	*moh-reh-TOHN*
bullet	bala	*BAH-lah*
bumper	defensa	*deh-FEHN-sah*
burgundy	guinda	*GEEN-dah*
burn	quemadura	*keh-mah-DOO-rah*
butcher	carnicero/a	*kahr-nee-SEH-roh/rah*

English	Spanish	Pronunciation
buttocks	glúteos	*gloo-TEH-obs*
Slang:	nalgas	*NAHL-gabs*
car	carro	*KAHR-rob*
	coche	*KOH-cheb*
	auto	*AU-oo-tob*
car insurance	seguro del carro	*seb-GOO-rob debl KAHR-rob*
cashier	cajero/a	*kab-HEH-rob/rab*
cat	gato	*GAH-tob*
child abuse	maltrato de niños	*mabl-TRAH-tob deb NEE-nyob*
children	niños	*NEE-nyobs*
Chilean	chileno/a	*chee-LEH-nob/nab*
Chinese	chino/a	*CHEE-nob/ab*
clothing store	tienda de ropa	*tee-EHN-dab deb ROH-pab*

continues

continued

English	Spanish	Pronunciation
cocaine	cocaína	*koh-kah-EE-nah*
Slang:	coca	*KOH-kah*
	perico	*peh-REE-koh*
	blanco	*BLAHN-koh*
	nieve	*nee-EH-veh*
	polvo	*POHL-voh*
	la huera	*lah oo-EH-rah*
Colombian	colombiano/a	*koh-lohm-bee-AH-noh/nah*
colored hair	teñido/pintado	*teh-NYEE-doh/peen-TAH-doh*
condominium	condominio	*kohn-doh-MEE-nee-oh*
construction	construcción	*kohn-strook-see-OHN*
contacts	lentes de contacto	*LEHN-tehs deh kohm-TAHK-toh*
copper (color)	cobre	*KOH-breh*
	cobrizo	*koh-BREE-soh*

English	Spanish	Pronunciation
Costa Rican	costarricense	*kohs-tahr-ree-SEHN-seh*
country	país	*pah-EES*
court	tribunal	*tree-BOO-nahl*
cousin, female	prima	*PREE-mah*
cousin, male	primo	*PREE-moh*
crack cocaine	piedra	*pee-EH-drah*
crime	delito	*deh-LEE-toh*
cry (v)	llorar	*yoh-RAHR*
Cuban	cubano/a	*koo-bah-noh/nah*
curly hair	pelo rizado	*PEH-loh ree-SAH-doh*
	pelo chino	*PEH-loh CHEE-noh*
damage	daño	*DAH-nyoh*
dance club	discoteca	*dees-koh-TEH-kah*

continues

continued

English	Spanish	Pronunciation
dark	oscuro	*ob-SKOO-rob*
dashboard	tablero del carro	*tab-BLEH-rob debl KAHR-rob*
daughter	hija	*EE-bab*
daughter-in-law	nuera	*noo-EH-rab*
day before yesterday	antes de ayer	*AHN-tebs deb ab-YEHR*
days	días	*DEE-abs*
December	diciembre	*dee-see-EHM-breb*
defendant, accused	acusado	*ab-coo-SAH-dob*
detain (v)	detener	*deb-teb-NEHR*
die (v)	fallecer	*fab-yeb-SEHR*
divorced	divorciado	*dee-vobr-see-AH-dob*
dog	perro	*PEHR-rob*
Dominican	dominicano/a	*dob-mee-nee-KAH-nob/nab*

English	Spanish	Pronunciation
drop it	suéltelo	*soo-EHL-teh-loh*
drugs	drogas	*DROH-gahs*
east	este	*EHS-teh*
Ecuadorian	ecuatoriano/a	*eh-kwah-toh-ree-AH-noh/nah*
ejaculate (v)	eyacular	*eh-yah-koo-LAHR*
Slang:	correrse	*kohr-rehr-SEH*
	venirse	*veh-neer-SEH*
elderly	ancianos/viejos	*ahn-see-AH-nohs/vee-EH-hohs*
emergency	emergencia	*eh-mehr-HEHN-see-ah*
employee	empleado/a	*ehm-pleh-AH-doh/dah*
escape (v)	escapar	*ehs-kah-PAHR*
evening	por la tarde	*pohr lah TAHR-deh*
ex-husband	ex-esposo	*ehx-ehs-POH-soh*

continues

continued

English	Spanish	Pronunciation
ex-wife	ex-esposa	*ehx-ehs-POH-sah*
extended cab	doble cabina	*DOH-bleh kah-BEE-nah*
fake identification	identificación falsa	*ee-dehn-tee-fee-kah-see-OHN FAHL-sah*
fat	gordo/panzón	*GOHR-doh/pahn-SOHN*
father	padre	*PAH-dreh*
father-in-law	suegro	*SWEH-groh*
February	febrero	*feh-BREH-roh*
feet	pies	*pee-EHS*
fender	guardafango	*gwahr-dah-FAHN-goh*
fictitious plates	placas falsas	*PLAH-kahs FAHL-sahs*
fine, monetary	multa	*MOOL-tah*
fingerprint	huella digital	*oo-EH-yah dee-bee-TAHL*

English	Spanish	Pronunciation
fingers	dedos	*DEH-dohs*
fire	fuego	*foo-EH-goh*
fist	puño	*POO-nyoh*
food store	mercado	*mehr-KAH-doh*
freckles	pecas	*PEH-kahs*
Friday	viernes	*vee-EHR-nehs*
friend, female	amiga	*ah-MEE-gah*
friend, male	amigo	*ah-MEE-goh*
gang	pandilla	*pahn-DEE-yah*
Slang:	ganga	*GAHN-gah*
gardener	jardinero	*hahr-dee-NEH-roh*
get out	salga	*SAHL-gah*

continues

continued

English	Spanish	Pronunciation
girlfriend	novia	*NOH-vee-ah*
glasses	lentes	*LEHN-tehs*
goatee	chivo/candado	*CHEE-voh/kahn-DAH-doh*
goddaughter	ahijada	*ah-ee-HAH-dah*
godson	ahijado	*ah-ee-HAH-doh*
gold (color)	dorado	*doh-RAH-doh*
gold (metal)	oro	*OH-roh*
granddaughter	nieta	*nee-EH-tah*
grandfather	abuelo	*ah-BWEH-loh*
grandmother	abuela	*ah-BWEH-lah*
grandson	nieto	*nee-EH-toh*
green	verde	*VEHR-deh*
gray	gris	*grees*

English	Spanish	Pronunciation
gray, dark	plomo	*PLOH-moh*
Guatemalan	guatemalteco/a	*goo-ah-teh-mahl-TEH-koh/kah*
hallucinogen	alucinógeno	*ah-loo-see-NOH-heh-noh*
handcuffs	esposas	*ehs-POH-sahs*
handgun		
Slang:	cuete	*koo-EH-teh*
	fierro	*fee-EHR-roh*
	fuca	*FOO-kah*
	fusca	*FOOS-kah*
handkerchief	pañuelo	*pah-NWEH-loh*
hands	manos	*MAH-nohs*
handsome	guapo	*goo-AH-poh*

continues

continued

English	Spanish	Pronunciation
headlights	luz delantera	*loos deh-lahn-TEH-rah*
	luz del frente	*loos dehl FREHN-teh*
heroin	heroína	*ehr-oh-EE-nah*
Slang:	negro	*NEH-groh*
	chiva	*CHEE-vah*
	cargada	*kahr-GAH-dah*
	llanta	*YAHN-tah*
hit (v)	golpear	*gohl-peh-AHR*
home	casa	*KAH-sah*
Honduran	hondureño/a	*ohn-doo-REH-nyoh/nyah*
hood of vehicle	cofre	*KOH-freh*
horse	caballo	*kah-BAH-yoh*

English	Spanish	Pronunciation
hurt (v)	lastimar	*labs-tee-MAHR*
husband	esposo	*eb-SPOH-sob*
	marido	*mab-REE-dob*
identification	identificación	*ee-debm-tee-fee-kab-see-OHN*
identify (v)	identificar	*ee-debm-tee-fee-KAHR*
ignition	arranque	*abr-RAHN-keb*
immigration	migración	*mee-grab-see-OHN*
infraction, traffic	infracción	*een-frabk-see-OHN*
inhalant	inhalante	*een-bab-LAHN-teb*
innocent	inocente	*ee-nob-SEHN-teb*
January	enero	*eb-NEH-rob*

continues

continued

English	Spanish	Pronunciation
Japanese	japonés/a	*hab-pob-NEHS/NEH-sab*
job	trabajo	*trab-BAH-bob*
Slang:	jale	*HAH-leb*
	chamba	*chabm-BAH*
July	julio	*HOO-lee-ob*
June	junio	*HOO-nee-ob*
key	llave	*YAH-veb*
kidnap (v)	secuestrar	*seb-kweb-STRAHR*
kidnapper	secuestrador	*seb-kweb-STRAH-dobr*
knee	rodilla	*rob-DEE-yab*
knife, household	cuchillo	*koo-CHEE-yob*
knife, hunting	cuchillo de caza	*koo-CHEE-yob deb KAH-sab*

continues

English	Spanish	Pronunciation
knife, kitchen	cuchillo de mesa	*koo-CHEE-ob deb MEH-sab*
knife, switchblade	navaja	*nah-VAH-hab*
Korean	coreano/a	*kob-reb-AH-nob/nab*
last night	anoche	*ah-NOH-cbeb*
Latin	latino/a	*lab-TEE-nob/nab*
law	ley	*leb*
left	izquierda	*ees-kee-EHR-dab*
leg	pierna	*pee-EHR-nab*
license	licencia	*lee-SEHN-see-ab*
license plate	placa	*PLAH-kab*
light-skinned person	güero/huero	*WEH-rob*
little (refers to a person)	chaparro	*cbab-PAHR-rob*

continued

English	Spanish	Pronunciation
long hair	pelo largo	*PEH-loh LAHR-goh*
look for (v)	buscar	*boos-KAHR*
loved one	querido	*keh-REE-doh*
machine gun	ametralladora	*ah-meh-trah-yah-DOH-rah*
	metralleta	*meh-trah-YEH-tah*
March	marzo	*MAHR-soh*
marijuana	marijuana	*mah-ree-boo-AH-nah*
Slang:	mota	*MOH-tah*
married	casado/casada	*kah-SAH-doh/kah-SAH-dah*
maternal last name	apellido materno	*ah-peh-YEE-doh mah-TEHR-noh*
May	mayo	*MAH-yoh*
meat store	carnicería	*kahr-nee-seh-REE-ah*

English	Spanish	Pronunciation
mechanic	mecánico	*meh-KAH-nee-koh*
medical attention	atención médica	*ah-tehn-see-OHN MEH-dee-kah*
medium	mediano	*meh-dee-AH-noh*
methamphetamine	metamfetamina	*meh-tahm-feh-tah-MEE-nah*
Slang:	cristal	*krees-TAHL*
	meta	*MEH-tah*
	G	*gee*
	vidrio	*VEE-dree-oh*
	hielo	*ee-EH-loh*
	ventana	*vehn-TAH-nah*
Mexican	mexicano/a	*meh-bee-KAH-noh/nah*
Mexican, U.S.-born	chicano/a	*chee-KAH-noh/nah*
	pocho/a	*POH-choh/chah*

continues

continued

English	Spanish	Pronunciation
	méxico-americano/a	*meh-bee-koh-ah-meh-ree-KAH-noh/nah*
mistreat (v)	maltratar	*mahl-trah-TAHR*
mole, face	lunar	*loo-NAH*
Monday	lunes	*LOO-nehs*
money	dinero	*dee-NEH-roh*
	feria	*feh-REE-ah*
months	meses	*MEH-sehs*
morning	mañana	*mah-NYAH-nah*
	en la mañana	*ehn lah mah-NYAH-nah*
	por la mañana	*pohr lah mah-NYAH-nah*
mother	madre	*MAH-dreh*
mother-in-law	suegra	*SWEH-grah*
motor	motor	*moh-TOHR*

English	Spanish	Pronunciation
motorcycle	moto	*MOH-toh*
move	muévase	*moo-EH-vah-seh*
muscular	musculoso	*moos-koo-LOH-soh*
mushrooms	hongos	*OHN-gohs*
mustache	bigote	*bee-GOH-teh*
name	nombre	*NOHM-breh*
nationality	nacionalidad	*nah-see-oh-nah-lee-DAHD*
neighbor	vecino	*veh-SEE-noh*
neighborhood	vecindario	*veh-seen-DAH-ree-oh*
nephew	sobrino	*soh-BREE-noh*
Nicaraguan	nicaragüense	*nee-kah-rah-GWEHN-seh*
nickname	apodo	*ah-POH-doh*
	sobrenombre	*soh-breh-NOHM-breh*

continues

continued

English	Spanish	Pronunciation
niece	sobrina	*soh-BREE-nah*
night	noche	*NOH-cheh*
north	norte	*NOHR-teh*
northeast	noreste	*nohr-EHS-teh*
northwest	noroeste	*nohr-oh-EHS-teh*
November	noviembre	*noh-vee-EHM-breh*
number	número	*NOO-meh-roh*
obstruct (v)	obstruir	*ohb-stroo-EER*
October	octubre	*ohk-TOO-breh*
officer	oficial	*oh-fee-SEE-ahl*
old	viejo	*vee-EH-hoh*
"old lady" (*slang*)	ruca	*ROO-kah*

continues

English	Spanish	Pronunciation
orange (color)	anaranjado	*ah-nah-rahn-HAH-doh*
orange (fruit)	naranja	*nah-RAHN-hah*
Panamanian	panameño/a	*pah-nah-MEH-nyoh/nyah*
Paraguayan	paraguayo/a	*pah-rah-goo-AH-yoh/yah*
passenger	pasajero	*pah-sah-HEH-roh*
passport	pasaporte	*pah-sah-POHR-teh*
paternal last name	apellido paterno	*ah-peh-YEE-doh pah-TEHR-noh*
patrol	patrulla	*pah-TROO-yah*
patrolman	patrullero	*pah-troo-YEH-roh*
patrolwoman	patrullera	*pah-troo-YEH-rah*
penis	pene	*PEH-neh*
Slang:	carajo	*kah-RAH-hoh*

continued

English	Spanish	Pronunciation
	nabo	*NAH-boh*
	piruli	*pee-ROO-lee*
	verga	*BEHR-gah*
Peruvian	peruano/a	*peh-roo-AH-noh/nah*
pharmacy	farmacia	*fahr-mah-SEE-ah*
Philippine	filipino/a	*fee-lee-PEE-noh/nah*
pick-up truck	camión	*kah-mee-OHN*
pink	rosa	*ROH-sah*
pipe	pipa	*PEE-pah*
pistol	pistola	*pees-TOH-lah*
police	policía	*poh-lee-SEE-ah*
Slang:	jura	*HOO-rah*
	chota	*CHOH-tah*

English	Spanish	Pronunciation
ponytail	cola/cola de caballo	*KOH-lah/KOH-lah deh kah-BAH-yoh*
pregnant	embarazada	*ehm-bah-rah-SAH-dah*
prescription drugs	recetas médicas	*reh-SEH-tahs MEH-dee-kahs*
Puerto Rican	puertorriqueño/a	*pwehr-toh-ree-KEH-nyoh/nyah*
pull	jale	*HAH-leh*
purple	morado	*moh-RAH-doh*
rain	lluvia	*YOO-vee-ah*
raise (v)	levantar	*leh-vahn-TAHR*
red	rojo	*ROH-hoh*
registration	registro, matrícula	*reh-HEE-stroh, mah-TREE-koo-lah*
registration, expired	registro vencido	*reh-HEE-stroh vehn-SEE-doh*

continues

continued

English	Spanish	Pronunciation
remove (v)	quitar	*kee-TAHR*
restaurant	restaurante	*rehs-tau-RAHN-teh*
right	derecha	*deh-REH-chah*
rob (v)	robar	*rob-BAHR*
rooster	gallo	*GAH-yoh*
rusty	oxidado	*ohx-ee-DAH-doh*
Salvadorian	salvadoreño/a	*sahl-vah-doh-reh-nyoh/nyah*
Saturday	sábado	*sah-BAH-doh*
scar	cicatriz	*see-KAH-treese*
scrape, "raspberry"	raspadura	*rahs-pah-DOO-rah*
scratch	arañazo	*ah-RAH-nyah-soh*
scratch	rasguño	*rahs-GOO-nyoh*

English	Spanish	Pronunciation
search warrant	orden de cateo	OHR-dehn deh KAH-teh-ob
seat	asiento	ab-see-EHN-tob
seat belt	cinto de seguridad	SEEN-tob deh seb-goo-ree-DAHD
semen	semen	SEH-mehn
Slang:	leche	LEH-cheb
	arroz con leche	abr-ROHS kobn LEH-cheb
semiautomatic	semiautomática	seb-mee-ab-tob-MAH-tee-kob
Slang:	cuadrada	kwab-DRAH-dab
September	septiembre	sebp-tee-EHM-breb
sex	tener relaciones sexuales	TEH-nehr reb-lab-see-OHN-ebs sebx-oo-AHL-ebs
Slang:	coger (v)	kob-HEHR
	costear (v)	kobs-teb-AHR
	culear (v)	koo-leb-AHR

continues

continued

English	Spanish	Pronunciation
sexual assault	violación	*vee-oh-lah-see-OHN*
short	bajo	*BAH-hoh*
short hair	pelo corto	*PEH-loh KOHR-toh*
shot, bullet wound	balazo	*bah-LAH-soh*
shotgun	escopeta	*ehs-koh-PEH-tah*
shut up	cállese	*KAH-yeh-seh*
sideburns	patillas	*pah-TEE-yahs*
silence	silencio	*see-lehn-SEE-oh*
silver (color)	plateado	*plah-teh-AH-doh*
silver (metal)	plata	*PLAH-tah*
sister	hermana	*ehr-MAH-nah*
sister-in-law	cuñada	*koo-NYAH-dah*
sit down	siéntese	*see-EHN-teh-seh*

continues

English	Spanish	Pronunciation
skin	piel	*pee-EHL*
skinny	flaco	*FLAH-koh*
slipper, sandal	chancla	*CHAHN-klah*
slow, slowly	despacio	*dehs-PAH-see-oh*
son	hijo	*EE-hoh*
son-in-law	yerno	*YEHR-noh*
south	sur	*soor*
southeast	sureste	*soor-EHS-teh*
southwest	suroeste	*soor-oh-EHS-teh*
Spanish	español/a	*ehs-pah-NYOHL/NYOH-lah*
spare tire	llanta de auxilio	*YAHN-tah deh aux-ee-LEE-oh*
speeding	exceso de velocidad	*ehx-SEH-soh deh veh-loh-SEE-dahd*
sport club	club deportivo	*cloob deh-pohr-TEE-voh*

continued

English	Spanish	Pronunciation
stand up	levántese	*leh-VAHN-teh-seh*
steering wheel	volante	*voh-LAHN-teh*
stick	palo	*PAH-loh*
stickers	calcomanías	*kahl-koh-mah-NEE-ahs*
stop sign	señal de alto	*seh-NYAHL deh AHL-toh*
store (small)	tienda	*tee-EHN-dah*
straight	derecho	*deh-REH-choh*
	lacio	*lah-SEE-oh*
straight hair	pelo lacio	*PEH-loh lah-SEE-oh*
strangle (v)	estrangular	*ehs-trahn-goo-LAHR*
street	calle	*KAH-yeh*
	carretera	*kahr-reh-TEH-rah*
Sunday	domingo	*doh-MEEN-goh*

English	Spanish	Pronunciation
supermarket	supermercado	*soo-pehr-mehr-KAH-doh*
suspect	sospechoso	*sohs-peh-CHOH-soh*
swearing in	jura	*HOO-rah*
taillight	luz trasera	*loos trah-SEH-rah*
tall	alto	*AHL-toh*
tattoo	tatuaje	*tah-too-AH-heh*
telephone number	número de teléfono	*NOO-meh-roh deh teh-LEH-foh-noh*
testicles	testículos	*tehs-TEE-koo-lohs*
Slang:	cojones	*koh-HOH-nehs*
	huevos	*oo-EH-vohs*
thin	delgado	*dehl-GAH-doh*
Thursday	jueves	*hoo-EH-vehs*

continues

continued

English	Spanish	Pronunciation
ticket	multa	*MOOL-tah*
tire	llanta	*YAHN-tah*
toe	dedo del pie	*DEH-dohs dehl pee-EH*
tow truck	grúa	*GROO-ah*
traffic infraction	infracción de tráfico	*een-frahk-see-OHN deh TRAH-fee-koh*
traffic lane	carril	*KAH-reel*
traffic light	semáforo	*seh-MAH-foh-roh*
trapped	atrapada	*ah-trah-PAH-dah*
trial	juicio	*boo-ee-SEE-oh*
trunk of vehicle	cajuela	*kah-hoo-WEH-lah*
Tuesday	martes	*MAHR-tehs*
turn around	voltéese	*vohl-TEH-eh-seh*
turn off (v)	apagar	*ah-pah-GAHR*

English	Spanish	Pronunciation
turning lights	luces de giro/direccional	*LOO-sehs deh HEE-roh/dee-rehk-see-oh-NAHL*
uncle	tío	*TEE-oh*
uniform	uniforme	*oo-nee-FOHR-meh*
Uruguayan	uruguayo/a	*oo-roo-goo-AH-yoh/yah*
vagina	vagina	*vah-HEE-nah*
Slang:	bacalao	*bah-kah-LAH-oo*
	panocha	*pah-NOH-chah*
	vulva	*VOOL-vah*
van	camioneta	*kah-mee-oh-NEH-tah*
vehicle	vehiculo	*veh-HEE-koo-loh*
Venezuelan	venezolano/a	*veh-neh-soh-LAH-noh/nah*

continues

continued

English	Spanish	Pronunciation
victim	víctima	*VEEK-tee-mah*
waiter	mesero	*meh-SEH-roh*
waitress	mesera	*meh-SEH-rah*
wavy hair	pelo ondulado	*PEH-loh ohn-doo-LAH-doh*
weapons	armas	*AHR-mahs*
Wednesday	miércoles	*mee-EHR-koh-lehs*
week	semana	*seh-MAH-nah*
well shaven	bien afeitado	*BEE-ehn ah-feh-TAH-doh*
west	oeste	*oh-EHS-teh*
white	blanco	*BLAHN-koh*
white person	gavacho	*gah-VAH-choh*
wife	esposa	*ehs-POH-sah*

English	Spanish	Pronunciation
windshield	vidrio	*VEE-dree-ob*
witness	testigo	*tebs-TEE-gob*
wound	herido	*eb-REE-dob*
yard	jardín	*babr-DEEN*
years	años	*AH-nyobs*
yellow	amarillo	*ab-mab-REE-yob*
yesterday	ayer	*ab-YEHR*
young	joven	*HOH-vebn*